INVINCIBLE

Torben Betts

INVINCIBLE

OBERON BOOKS
LONDON

WWW.OBERONBOOKS.COM

First published in 2014 by Oberon Books Ltd
521 Caledonian Road, London N7 9RH
Tel: +44 (0) 20 7607 3637 / Fax: +44 (0) 20 7607 3629
e-mail: info@oberonbooks.com
www.oberonbooks.com

A catalogue record for this book is available from the British
Library.

PB ISBN: 978-1-78319-110-9
E ISBN: 978-1-78319-609-8

Cover image by Tom Crowley

for Sam Walters

with thanks for your support over the last thirteen years
and with very best wishes for your retirement from the Orange Tree

Characters

EMILY

OLIVER

DAWN

ALAN

The play is set over several months of a recent summer and takes place in EMILY and OLIVER's living room and kitchen area. There are various examples of Emily's abstract artwork hanging in the living room. There is also a baby monitor in a prominent position, i.e on a coffee table.

Location: a small town (or suburb)
in the north of England.

All characters mid-30s plus.

Invincible was first performed on 12 March 2014 at the Orange Tree Theatre, Richmond with the following cast:

EMILY	Laura Howard
OLIVER	Darren Strange
DAWN	Samantha Seager
ALAN	Daniel Copeland

Director, Ellie Jones
Designer, Sam Dowson
Lighting Designer, John Harris
Trainee Director, Sophie Boyce
Assistant Design, Katy Mills
Stage Manager, Stuart Burgess
Deputy Stage Manager, Sophie Acreman
Assistant Stage Managers, Becky Flisher and Poppy Walker
Production Technician, Tim Bifield

Production Photographer, Robert Day

Invincible transferred to St. James Theatre as a co-production with the Orange Tree Theatre and was first performed on 10 July 2014 with the following cast:

EMILY	Laura Howard
OLIVER	Darren Strange
DAWN	Samantha Seager
ALAN	Daniel Copeland

Director, Ellie Jones
Designer, Sam Dowson
Lighting Designer, Tim Mascall
Assistant Director, Sophie Boyce
Associate Costume Designer, Katy Mills

Production Manager, Lee Batty
Stage Manager, Annie Kalinauckas
Deputy Stage Manager, Allie Hook

Act One

The floor is littered with toys, jigsaw puzzles etc. After a time we hear offstage voices.

OLIVER: …because I just don't see what difference it would make…

EMILY: It would make a big difference to me so…

OLIVER: But wouldn't it just be a really…

EMILY: 'Nice' thing to do?

OLIVER: A really nice thing to do, yes.

EMILY: But I don't believe in it so…

OLIVER: I know you don't *believe* in it but…

EMILY: *(Now on, straight into tidying away the toys etc.)* So you keep on asking me to do something that offends my whole…

OLIVER: *(Also now on.)* 'Offends' is a bit strong surely…?

EMILY: Well, it *does* offend my…

OLIVER: It *doesn't* offend your…

EMILY: Please don't tell me what does and what does not offend my…

OLIVER: Not *really.*

EMILY: What does and does not offend my…

OLIVER: I don't know why you always have to be so…

EMILY: I'm not being so…

OLIVER: Why you always have to be so…

EMILY: You have always known my position on…

OLIVER: Yes, but Mum is dying now, isn't she? She's dying now and when I've suggested it before she *wasn't* dying so…

EMILY: And I'm not going through with something I don't believe in simply to be…

OLIVER: Kind?

EMILY: It's not a question of kindness, is it, it just goes against my principles…

OLIVER: To please someone who may only have six months to live. It's just a ceremony. It's just a…

EMILY: Surely she's got more important things on her mind than you and I engaging in some mediaeval exercise in…

OLIVER: All I'm asking you to do is…

EMILY: I've offered to have her here while she…

OLIVER: I'm not asking you to get married in a church!

EMILY: I'm happy to care for her, to nurse her…

OLIVER: Although that would please her more than you could poss…

EMILY: I'll do everything I can for her, to make her final days as happy and as peaceful as…

OLIVER: I know and I'm extremely grateful but…

EMILY: She can come here. I'll devote myself to her, I'll support you, I'll…

OLIVER: I know, I know…

EMILY: But marriage is an institution based on…

OLIVER: But it's *me*. You'd be marrying *me*. I'm not going to possess you. I'm not going to suddenly chain you to the sink and prevent you from having…

EMILY: The woman doesn't even approve of me.

OLIVER: I love you so much, Emily, and all I want is for us to…

EMILY: I've tried and I've tried but we just don't get on.

OLIVER: She means well.

EMILY: Another conversation we have that just goes…

OLIVER: She's just a bit set in her ways.

EMILY: …round and round and…

OLIVER: She just likes things to be done in a certain…

EMILY: 'A *bit* set in her ways?'

OLIVER: All I want, if I can, is to make her final days as…

EMILY: She's a bigoted, right-wing, Christian fundamentalist…

OLIVER: She's hardly a fundamentalist!

They do not speak as she continues preparing for their guests.

You do realise, when she does eventually go, you do realise our financial situation may well become a little less precarious?

EMILY: I've told you, I'm not interested in any of her ill-gotten…

OLIVER: For God's sake…

EMILY: We need to maintain our independence.

OLIVER: And *of course* she approves of you.

EMILY: Inherited wealth is just another way of perpetuating…

OLIVER: You're the mother of her grandchildren for one thing…

EMILY: What does that mean?

OLIVER: It means that you're very…

EMILY: That does…that statement does in fact define my sole function as far as she's concerned so…

OLIVER: She just thinks you're still a bit…

EMILY: I am *not* highly-strung!

OLIVER: I wasn't even going to say…

EMILY: I know she thinks I'm highly-strung.

OLIVER: You know how much she respects you.

EMILY: Respects?!

OLIVER: But she *is*, like I am, like all of us are, she *is* still allowed to be concerned about your mental and your emotional…

EMILY: She thinks I should just get over it!

OLIVER: Oh, of course she doesn't!

EMILY: 'It's been four years so the silly girl should just jolly well pull herself together.'

OLIVER: She doesn't even talk like that.

EMILY: 'We grew up during a war. People died every day back then.'

OLIVER: You make her sound like some character from a…

EMILY: Hold on!

OLIVER: And you know she doesn't think that for a second.

She listens closely to the baby monitor, examines it.

EMILY: Think I heard the baby…

OLIVER: I didn't hear…

EMILY: We really need to get one with a camera.

OLIVER: She *is* two and a half. She's hardly a baby…

EMILY: I just think she's still quite…

OLIVER: Come on, they're both perfectly…

EMILY: Listen, I haven't stopped all day so would you please just…

OLIVER: She'll be fast asleep so…

EMILY: Please, Oliver. Will you please just check on her?

With a sigh he leaves.

She busies herself, preparing. Stops. Has a word with herself. Tries to calm down. She then goes to the bookshelves, selects some books and puts a few on the coffee table, rearranges them, puts out bowls of nuts, olives etc.

She checks her watch, puts some music on (James Brown's 'Living in America') then continues. After a time it annoys her and we soon hear the Sanctus from William Byrd's mass for five voices.

The singing takes an effect. EMILY stands still, head down, calming herself, closing her eyes, performing metta.

May I be free from danger. May I have mental happiness. May I have physical health. May I live my life at ease. May I be free from danger. May I have mental happiness.

OLIVER returns. He watches her.

May I have physical health. May I live my life at ease.

OLIVER: He's reading *Asterix.*

She holds up a hand.

And she's snoring like a pig.

EMILY: May my enemies be free from danger. May they have mental happiness. May they have physical health. May they live their lives at ease.

She finishes.

OLIVER: Better?

She smiles at him. She then resumes her preparations in a noticeably more relaxed manner.

By the way, have you seen that flag?

EMILY: What flag?

OLIVER: Number 52. There's now yet another flag of St George beautifying the street. Almost covers their whole…

EMILY: *(Losing her new-found calm.)* Oh, why, why, why do people always have to make the world so bloody ugly!

OLIVER: I think it's either the World Cup or the European…

EMILY: If there's one thing I can't stand then it's…

OLIVER: Mindless patriotism?

EMILY: Is there any other variety?

OLIVER: I think we're now the only remaining flag-free members of this…

EMILY: A beautiful street of nineteenth-century stone and human beings in their infinite wisdom somehow manage to… Oh, I don't know.

They do not speak for a time. He sits and picks up one of the books on the coffee table ('Das Kapital' by Karl Marx). Examines it. The music plays on.

OLIVER: You think they'll appreciate, who is it, Thomas Tallis?

EMILY: It's William Byrd.

OLIVER: You think they'll appreciate William Byrd?

EMILY: Who knows, my darling, or even dares to dream?

They do not speak for a time.

OLIVER: All sounds the same.

EMILY: Indeed it does not.

OLIVER: All this dreary, polyphonic…

EMILY: William Byrd is quite different from Thomas Tallis.

OLIVER: No, he isn't.

EMILY: I'm afraid he is.

OLIVER: Would you swear to that in a court of law?

EMILY: And it's not remotely dreary.

OLIVER: If you say so.

EMILY: William Byrd is much more… Thomas Tallis is far less…

OLIVER: Well, now that you've explained it to me with such….

EMILY: Byrd is far more Catholic for a start.

OLIVER: So what does Catholicism sound like?

EMILY: It sounds exactly like this.

They listen to the singing for a time.

Do you have any idea how brave this man was in an age when Catholics were hunted down and…

OLIVER: I never knew you were so sympathetic towards…

EMILY: I am sympathetic, Oliver, towards the oppressed.

OLIVER: I know you are.

EMILY: Towards any individual who is ever bullied by the state.

They listen on.

There's a massive difference.

They do not speak for a time. She takes in the music. Seems on the verge of tears. Turns from him.

OLIVER: Listen, can I ask you something?

EMILY: *(Resuming tidying etc.)* Sounds ominous…

OLIVER: And you have to promise me you won't get all…

EMILY: How can I promise you I won't get all…?

OLIVER: All I mean is…

EMILY: Whatever you ask me might perfectly easily make me get all…

OLIVER: I just don't want you to…you know… I'd prefer it if tonight you could possibly refrain from… All I'm saying is that I'm hoping you might just…

EMILY: Spit it out, Oliver, for God's sake!

OLIVER: I just don't want you to mention their cat.

EMILY: I'm not going to mention their cat!

OLIVER: You say that but…

EMILY: Why do you assume I am going to mention their…

OLIVER: Because their cat really gets on your tits.

EMILY: It does get on my tits, correct!

OLIVER: And I don't want you to mention it.

EMILY: It really, *really* gets on my tits in fact!

OLIVER: And you do have, it has to be said, a really fantastic pair of tits.

She stops what she's doing and glowers at him.

What?

EMILY: What an unbelievably infantile thing to say.

OLIVER: I'm sorry.

She continues in silent anger.

Oh, come on. I was only being…

EMILY: And if I'd wanted some ghastly, bird-murdering brute crapping on my courgettes and terrifying my children's guinea pigs half to death and making sure precisely no greenfinch, no robin, no tit, not even a bloody sparrow ever comes within half a mile of all my feeders out there then I would of course have got one for myself…

OLIVER: There's nothing we can do, is there?

EMILY: This morning the bastard was vomiting all over the oregano!

OLIVER: But there's nothing we can do!

EMILY: Lion piss!

OLIVER: Excuse me?

EMILY: You can buy lion urine online. It's extremely expensive but it scares them away apparently.

OLIVER: Right. Good. So. Lion piss it is then.

He flips through the book.

EMILY: See, I didn't get remotely all…

OLIVER: Well, no, you didn't get particularly…

EMILY: I have remained perfectly calm.

OLIVER: And so you promise you won't mention it?

EMILY: I already told you…

They do not speak for a time as she tidies.

OLIVER: What's his name again?

EMILY: Alan or Adam or…

OLIVER: And what does he do?

EMILY: Eats with enthusiasm by the look of him.

OLIVER: No, I've seen him. He's a postman.

EMILY: Well, those guys are being well and truly stabbed in the back. They should all be out on strike.

They do not speak for a time as she tidies.

OLIVER: Listen…what happened this morning. I mean, the argument we had this morning. Can I just say that…

EMILY: Well, I'm sorry I bit your head off but…

OLIVER: No, *I'm* sorry.

EMILY: Seriously, it's *me* who should be sorry.

OLIVER: Well, we still need to talk about it.

EMILY: Yes, but not now.

OLIVER: Sorry, but you always say that.

EMILY: I always say what?

OLIVER: You always say not now.

EMILY: We've got the locals coming round!

OLIVER: I know but wherever we are or whatever we're doing you always say not now.

EMILY: I'm sorry but I'm not talking about our sex life immediately…

OLIVER: Our *lack* of sex life…

EMILY: I am not talking about our lack of sex life immediately prior to…

OLIVER: But when *do* we talk about it?

EMILY: We don't talk about it now!

OLIVER: Because it *is* becoming an issue.

EMILY: Anyway I'm trying to move beyond sex.

OLIVER: I beg your pardon?

EMILY: Hold on a minute!

She examines the monitor again.

Will you go and check on her please?

OLIVER: What did you just say?

EMILY: I definitely heard something.

OLIVER: Well, *you* go and check on her then!

She looks at him. Then leaves.

He remains. Despairs to the heavens as Byrd's singers continue.

SCENE 2

The singing continues: the Agnus Dei. OLIVER and DAWN. They do not speak for a time.

OLIVER: So, yes I… I think, well, I *hope* she'll be down in a minute.

DAWN says nothing. Only the singing.

She's just checking on the…the kids. *(A beat.)* Again. We've got two. Two kids. Two children.

DAWN says nothing. Only the singing.

What do you make of William Byrd then?

DAWN: Who's he?

OLIVER: Well, he's the man who came up with this…this cheery little ditty.

DAWN: Sort of makes you wanna kill yourself, dunnit?

OLIVER: Top of the Pops in 1595 apparently.

DAWN: Is that a fact?

OLIVER: I can easily… I mean, I'm more than happy to… More than happy to put something else on if you'd…

She walks about. He watches her for a time with awkward desire.

And you have two daughters, I believe?

DAWN: Couple who lived here before you…

OLIVER: Yes?

DAWN: Jesus Christ.

OLIVER: I see.

DAWN: The husband…he had a proper twinkle in his eye.

OLIVER: Did he indeed?

DAWN: Indeed he did.

They stare at each other until he looks away.

OLIVER: Well, I suppose that's… Well. Yes. Jolly good.

He coughs nervously. They do not speak. She walks about some more.

DAWN: What's your wife's name again?

OLIVER: Oh, she's not my wife.

DAWN: Not your wife?

OLIVER: We're not married.

DAWN: Why's that then?

OLIVER: To be honest, I don't really know.

DAWN: But you got kids together?

OLIVER: We do.

DAWN: But you're not wed?

OLIVER: Em doesn't really believe in it.

DAWN: Sounds like she's got her head screwed on then.

They do not speak. She looks around.

OLIVER: We're still in mid-embellishment actually.

DAWN: You what?

OLIVER: The owner's given us a free rein to, you know, put our little stamp on it so…

DAWN: It's not your house then?

OLIVER: My partner doesn't believe in private property. As a concept.

DAWN: She doesn't believe in a lot of things.

OLIVER: Well, no…

DAWN: Never had your sort here before…you know, living in this street. All the posh folk, they tend to live on the other side of town.

OLIVER: Well, Emily just felt that… Sorry, *we* just felt that we wanted our kids to grow up among what she calls 'real people' and with more of a sense of…

DAWN: Real people?

OLIVER: Real people, yes.

They do not speak.

So…you're a working mother, I do believe?

DAWN: At the dental clinic.

OLIVER: So you're a receptionist then…?

DAWN: Smart lad.

OLIVER: One does try one's best.

DAWN: Cut me hours last year though. Only part-time now. Bored stupid for three hours a day instead of eight.

OLIVER: Well, I think all jobs do tend to get a tad…a tad tedious after a while, don't they?

DAWN: 'A tad tedious'?

OLIVER: A tad tedious, yes.

He coughs nervously. She smiles to herself.

DAWN: So what's yours then? Your job that's 'a tad tedious'?

OLIVER: Well, almost since I left university I've worked for the Civil Service. In an editorial capacity. Sat behind a desk all day essentially, behind a computer screen and then along come Mr Recession and Mr Cuts and Yours Truly is ushered very discreetly towards the exit. Got a half-decent pay-off but we couldn't really afford the rent on a family home in London any longer so we…we relocated up here. So to speak. Em's grandfather hailed from a village not far away so she has fond childhood memories of the area but otherwise it was just emigrating anywhere we could be under less financial pressure, so to speak, what with my unfortunate drop in earnings and the far more reasonable rents in this part of the world and so now I do a bit of freelance work from home and Em is in the process of setting up an artists' co-operative along with forming a local Amnesty group and so she wanted…well, *we* wanted, sorry, we wanted to live a different kind of life, you know, away from the stresses and the strains of the city and anyway she has always maintained that London is, and I quote, 'a hideous capitalistic gangbang' and, yes, we wanted the kids to grow up with more of a sense of nature and with more of a sense of community and we also wanted to live our lives on a smaller, more human scale but…

DAWN: You talk a lot, don't you?

OLIVER: Sorry…

They do not speak for a time.

Can I…can I offer you a cup of tea at all?

DAWN: A cup of what?

OLIVER: I'm afraid we have no alcohol.

DAWN: You're taking the piss?

OLIVER: We're not great drinkers in this house.

DAWN: I'll wait for Al then. He's bringing some cans.

An awkward silence.

He talks a lot an'all. Like a prattling old woman.

OLIVER: So, sorry…your husband will be joining us shortly, will he?

DAWN: When the football's finished.

OLIVER: I see.

DAWN: England are playing.

OLIVER: Oh, it's tonight, is it?

DAWN: You don't like football?

OLIVER: Loathe it actually.

DAWN: So do I.

OLIVER: Hate it.

DAWN: Despise it.

OLIVER: Abhor it.

They look at each other. He looks away.

Always been more of a cricket man.

DAWN: You know what: I reckon you might be my kind of
bloke.

OLIVER: Oh, really?

DAWN: You talk posh, you like posh music, you read posh
books and you don't like football.

The sexual tension builds. EMILY now on.

EMILY: So sorry about that. She's quite restless in the evenings
these days and I do like to… Anyway, welcome, welcome.
I'm Emily and it's Dawn, isn't it?

DAWN: That's right.

An awkward silence.

EMILY: And so is your husband not here or…?

OLIVER: He's watching the football.

EMILY: Oh, I see.

DAWN: Be over when it's over.

OLIVER: England are playing.

DAWN: Never misses an England game.

EMILY: Well, okay then. Not to worry.

An awkward silence.

OLIVER: Yes, we're not really…not really football people in
this house, I'm afraid.

DAWN: You said.

An awkward silence.

OLIVER: Always been more of a…

DAWN: Cricket man?

OLIVER: That's right.

22

An awkward silence.

If I might run the risk of blowing my own trumpet for a second: I was for a time a professional. As a younger man.

No response.

People often say that to look at me I don't much…people don't tend to equate me with professional sport. I don't have that demeanour apparently but I used to play all the time. I was a pretty good bowler as a matter of fact. Bit of an all-rounder to be truthful. I was also very good at fielding.

No response.

I was very accurate with my throws. Over long distances. Strange skill to have but there you go. Must have been some evolutionary adaptation I inherited. You know, early man lobbing stones at antelope and what have you.

Nobody speaks for a time.

EMILY: Sorry, so what time will he actually be here then?

DAWN: Like I said, when it's over.

EMILY: I see.

They do not speak for a time.

OLIVER: So, Dawn. How long have you lived in this town?

DAWN: Born and bred on this street.

OLIVER: Right.

DAWN: In a house just across the road.

They do not speak for a time.

EMILY: And so…might I ask: do you like the area or…?

DAWN: Sorry, can I use your bog?

EMILY: I beg your pardon?

OLIVER: It's through there, up the stairs, first on your left.

DAWN: Ta very much.

DAWN leaves.

EMILY and OLIVER regard each other for a time.

EMILY: She's hardly wearing any clothing!

OLIVER: It's just a different culture.

EMILY: But we're all English, aren't we?

OLIVER: I know but…

EMILY: And it might be more pleasant for me if you refrained from ogling her in that manner…

OLIVER: I wasn't ogling her.

EMILY: Oliver, I'm not blind.

OLIVER: I definitely wasn't ogling her. I don't ogle. I'm not an ogler.

EMILY: You were ogling her.

OLIVER: I mean, she's an attractive woman but…

EMILY: But you don't need to ogle her.

OLIVER: I wasn't!

EMILY: And what's that all about? You accept an invitation to meet your new neighbours who are going out of their way to be friendly and sociable and you're given a time and a date and instead of…

OLIVER: He'll be here when the football's…

EMILY: Instead of arriving at the agreed…

OLIVER: It's not that important…

EMILY: You just turn up whenever you…

OLIVER: England are playing.

He watches her.

Please. Emily. You're getting all…

EMILY: I'm not remotely getting all…

OLIVER: Let's just try to relax and have a pleasant evening and…

EMILY: I *am* relaxed.

OLIVER: You're *not* relaxed.

EMILY: Plus: I just saw their cat again…

OLIVER: Okay, but…

EMILY: Just sat there, watching the guinea pigs, stalking them, just waiting to…

OLIVER: But that's what cats do.

EMILY: No wonder those rodents have become so neurotic.

OLIVER: It's just obeying its nature.

EMILY: Not in my bloody garden it isn't.

DAWN now returns.

DAWN: I love your bedroom up there by the way. I'd love to have an en suite like that. Sick and tired of sharing a bathroom with the girls. We were going to try and build one in but Alan earns next to nothing and they've cut my hours so that was that idea bolloxed before it even started. So, what, you don't have any booze at all? You two a pair of alcoholics or what?

EMILY and OLIVER, smile awkwardly, exchange looks.

SCENE 3

ALAN, who is a very large and cheerful man, stands with a can of lager in his hand, resplendent in England football shirt. He is a little merry. The others in attendance, DAWN also with a can.

ALAN: So, as I say, our main problem is we just don't know how to keep the ball. If you look at your Spains, your Italys, your Germanys, or your top South American sides, then the one thing they can all do much better than us is, as I say: Keep the Ball. It's Pass and Move and Pass and Move and Play the Ball To Feet because, at the end of the day, football is a simple game, intit? It's keep the ball, work your way into scoring positions and then try and stick more in the net than the opposition do. And, as I say, it starts when you're a kid, you know, 'cos we all did it at school, didn't we, we're all just tearing around

after the ball or we're just hoofing it up the pitch and
scrambling after it like a load of headless chickens and,
as I say, we're not taught how to keep it, you know,
one-touch football or two-touch football, and so, as I say,
you've got to drum it into their heads when they're five,
six, seven years of age: Keep the Ball, lads! Let the Ball
Do the Work, Pass and Move, Pass and Move, Keep it on
the Deck. And so when it comes to your World Cups or
your European Championships, then our national sides
are always outclassed. So tonight, as I say, the quality of
the football were abysmal. Hard to keep your eyes on the
screen it were that dull. We got one, maybe two world-class
players but, as I say, other than that… Dawn'll tell you, up
until recently, me and the lads would travel all over the
place to follow England. Sadly I can't afford it now 'cos
it's an expensive hobby but, as I say, I've been all over the
place: France, Denmark, Italy, Poland, Greece, Portugal,
Switzerland, Austria, Finland, San Marino, Italy…

DAWN: You already said Italy!

ALAN: You what?

DAWN: We get the idea, thank you.

ALAN: I'm just talking…

DAWN: You're *always* talking.

ALAN: *(Laughing.)* Sorry, she's always telling me: Alan, you
talk too much.

DAWN: That's because you *do*…

ALAN: She's always on at me like she says Alan you know
what your biggest problem is and I says no Dawn you tell
me what *is* my biggest problem and she says you talk too
much so I'm sorry if I do, I mean you'll just have to say,
you'll have to say, sorry pal but I don't know if you know it
but you might just be talking a bit too much at the moment
and then I'll try and put a lid on it. See, me mum, she had
a right mouth on her, Christ she would talk and talk and
talk and talk and it used to send my dear old Dad round
the bend so the poor sod lived most of his life hiding in

his shed at the bottom of the garden and so if I have got it from her I don't really know but...

DAWN: Thank you!

ALAN: Now, the girls, *our* girls, that's Megan and Sophie, they *never* stop talking and Dawn's always going you're as bad as they are and I go Jesus Christ I hope that's not the case, I hope to God I don't talk as much as they do because in that case life would be awful for her, for Dawn here and see, she's not like me. See, I'm always going, aren't I, I'm always going Dawn, Dawn, please will you say something, please will you speak please because I never ever know what the bloody hell you're thinking...

DAWN: You don't want to know what I'm thinking right now.

ALAN: *(Laughing.)* Do I not?

DAWN: No, you do not.

ALAN's laugh dies away and then nobody speaks for a time. He swigs from his can.

EMILY: We have a glass if you...

ALAN: No thanks, love. I'm an Out the Can Man.

EMILY: Right.

ALAN: Always been an Out the Can Man. *(To DAWN.)* Haven't I?

No response. DAWN and ALAN swig from their cans. The awkward silence builds.

OLIVER: So... Alan...

ALAN: You not watch the footie then, pal?

DAWN: He prefers cricket.

ALAN: Don't understand cricket so...

DAWN: Well, *he* does.

ALAN: It's just blokes in white standing about all day, intit?

DAWN: Oliver was a professional.

ALAN: No way?

OLIVER: Well, semi-professional really but…

ALAN: Jesus, pal, that's… I can't believe it.

ALAN goes to OLIVER and shakes his hand vigorously.

Who you play for?

OLIVER: Middlesex for a couple of seasons. On and off. After I left university. But I was always…

ALAN: That's brilliant.

OLIVER: Wasn't a regular or anything but…

ALAN: No, seriously: I am well impressed with that.

Nobody speaks for a time.

You like sport, love?

EMILY: I happen to think that highly popular sports like football are nowadays merely a means of keeping people pacified, of keeping people stupid. The more time, money and energy a man spends watching football, for example, the less time, money and energy he has to read important books and to educate himself and to question this hideous economic system and therefore, one hopes, to realise he's being taken for a fool every single day of his life.

ALAN and DAWN exchange looks.

ALAN: Okey-dokey…

EMILY: An obsession with competitive sport doesn't improve the soul or the mind of anyone. In fact it does the opposite: it rots the soul.

ALAN: Just want to feel like I belong, Emily.

EMILY: Yes, but belong to what exactly?

Awkward silence.

OLIVER: My partner, you will note, is something of a contrarian.

ALAN: *(Laughing.)* Don't worry, pal! We don't care what religion she is!

He laughs wildly. No one else does. The laughter dies away.

28

EMILY: I find that rather insulting to be honest.

OLIVER: I didn't meant to insult you.

EMILY: You're implying that I say these things purely to be…

OLIVER: Listen, thank you both so much for coming.

They do not speak for a time.

I tend to think it's always wise to keep things like politics and religion out of…

EMILY: Oliver, if we're not allowed to discuss…

OLIVER: All I'm saying is…

EMILY: What *are* we allowed to talk about then if we can't…

ALAN: Tell you what, the couple who lived here before you… Jesus Christ.

EMILY: I'm not sure I follow, sorry?

DAWN: No class at all.

ALAN: Lived next door for, what, seven, eight year. Barely spoke a word.

EMILY: That's a shame.

ALAN: Trouble was: the bloke, he really fancied this one.

DAWN: Alright!

ALAN: *(Laughing.)* Well, he did!

DAWN: Okay but…

ALAN: It's hardly surprising, is it? Just look at her. She's proper gorgeous, in't she? Proper, proper gorgeous. Most people take one look at me and they go how did a big fat slob like him manage to land a spectacular-looking woman like her? And I do ask meself the same question, I have to be honest, because she is stunning, in't she? And every day I thank whoever it is up there you're supposed to thank, I say, thank God, I managed to land a beautiful woman like this. I'm the envy of the whole town, you know, always have been, because she's like a supermodel, in't she?

DAWN: Alan!

ALAN: And she's got to the ripe old age of thirty-something and she's knocked out three kids and still she looks like a million dollars and of course I didn't always look like this, in me twenties I were pretty trim of course but what would you say, pal? She is absolutely gorgeous, in't she, don't you think, this woman here is one hundred and ten per cent absolutely bloody bleeding gorgeous?

No response at first.

I'm waiting, Oliver!

DAWN: For God's sake!

OLIVER: Well, yes. She is of course an extremely...

ALAN: Don't you think she's one of the most sexiest women you've ever seen in your whole...

EMILY: Sorry, would either of you care for an olive?

ALAN/DAWN: No ta.

OLIVER takes one.

They do not speak for a time.

EMILY: Thank you so much for coming.

ALAN: Nice to be asked.

Nobody speaks for a time.

EMILY: We did also invite the old lady on the other side but sadly she neglected to respond.

DAWN: Mrs Montgomery?

ALAN: She were our teacher as it goes.

DAWN: She were an evil old bitch.

ALAN: Oh, she were alright.

DAWN: She still is.

ALAN: Used to teach us maths.

DAWN: Science.

ALAN: Keeps herself to herself now.

EMILY: Well, she has an immaculate lawn.

ALAN: Vince is always winding up her Siamese so we don't really speak…

EMILY: And so Vince is your son, yes?

ALAN bursts out laughing.

DAWN: No. Vince is not our…

ALAN: He's me cat!

ALAN is unable to stop laughing as the others watch.

OLIVER: Would anyone care to take a pew or…?

ALAN: I say '*my* cat' because Dawn here's never…

DAWN: I hate the little bugger.

EMILY: God, so do I.

ALAN: *(Stops laughing.)* You what?

A silence.

OLIVER: What she means is she's not really a cat person.

DAWN: The girls completely love him so I put up with him but otherwise…

ALAN: Vince is me best bloody mate!

Nobody speaks for a time.

EMILY: Sorry, I'm just a little confused: he mentioned you had 'knocked out', I think that was the expression he employed, had 'knocked out' *three* children so is your other child grown up now because you barely seem old enough to…?

ALAN: We have a son.

EMILY: So you had him when you were very young, did you?

ALAN: She finished school on the Friday. Knocked him out on the Tuesday.

EMILY: So…he's away at college now or…?

ALAN: He's just…away.

A long silence.

OLIVER: So…do your daughters go to St Margaret's then?

ALAN: That's right.

EMILY: And they manage…?

ALAN: They hold their own.

EMILY: Yes, well, when we had a tour last week the classrooms did seem a little…lively.

ALAN: *(Laughing.)* You mean, out of control?

OLIVER: Our son, who is ten, is rather sensitive so we're a tad concerned about…

DAWN: If he starts at St Margaret's then he won't be sensitive for long.

ALAN: You could always send him to the Towers.

OLIVER: We *have* discussed it.

EMILY: We don't believe in private education.

OLIVER: Well, *you* don't but…

ALAN: Costs an arm and a leg, mind.

EMILY: It's appallingly unjust and it has a deleterious effect on a child's character.

OLIVER: Well, I had a private education and it didn't do me any harm.

EMILY: That of course is a matter of opinion.

DAWN: I'd kill to send the girls there. Give them a fighting chance at least.

OLIVER: Well, it is a sad fact of life in this country that if you do want your kids educated to any reasonable standard then you do generally have to pay through the nose for…

EMILY: Perpetuating the stranglehold the rich have always had over the….

OLIVER: Then let's home school them.

EMILY: Who's going to do that?

OLIVER: Well, I really don't have the time so…

EMILY: And neither do I.

OLIVER: Well, we can think about it at a later date perhaps.

EMILY: It's up to intelligent, well-educated people like ourselves to stay and help improve these failing local schools which is why I've applied to be on the Board of Governors.

They do not speak for a time.

ALAN: Okay-dokey. Think I might just go and refuel, like.

ALAN goes to get another lager. On stage a silence until:

OLIVER: Shall we sit Dawn? Down. I apologise, sorry...shall we sit down, Dawn?

DAWN smiles to herself and sits. She picks up the Marx.

EMILY: Do you know his work at all?

DAWN: Can't say I do.

Nobody speaks. An awkward silence descends.

I like your dress.

EMILY: Thank you.

OLIVER: She made it herself.

DAWN: I'm impressed.

The silence builds.

Do the odd bit of knitting meself.

EMILY: Oh really?

DAWN: Helps keep me off the fags, you know.

ALAN back with his lager. Nobody speaks. He picks up the book.

ALAN: I do quite like some of them old-style comedians like Harold Lloyd and Buster Keaton and the Chaplin one when he gets stuck in all that machinery but the Marx Brothers I just don't get. I just don't get the jokes to be fair, and it's too fast for me, too clever-clever and, as I say, they don't even begin to get anywhere near my absolute all-time one hundred and fifty per cent favourites who are, wait for it, wait for it: Mr Stanley Laurel and Mr Oliver Norvell Hardy.

DAWN: You've had too much to drink, mate.

ALAN: In the 1930s, see, everyone in the world was suffering. The Great Depression and everything. People were starving. No jobs, no food, no housing. And these two guys, right, these two guys put smiles on the faces of millions. Spread laughter and happiness at a time when folk were really struggling.

EMILY: I believe entertainment at that time was actually used very deliberately as a means of taking people's attention away from the fact that the Wall Street speculators had single-handedly stripped...

ALAN: They made the people happy.

DAWN: Oh, for God's sake please don't treat them to your...

ALAN now embarks on a very poor Oliver Hardy impression: the nervous laugh, the tie fiddle etc.

ALAN: 'Well, here's another nice mess you've gotten me into.'

ALAN now laughs starts to laugh uncontrollably, watched in silence by the others. He is unable to stop laughing and is soon doubled up, gasping for breath.

SCENE 4

ALAN, looking at the paintings, and OLIVER.

OLIVER: So you're a postman then?

ALAN: *(Singing.)* "Stop, oh yes, wait a minute, Mr Postman!

ALAN laughs, stops, waits for a reaction. Doesn't get one.

Used to do a bit of singing, as it goes.

OLIVER: Right.

ALAN: It were a real...passion.

They do not speak for a time as ALAN continues to look at the paintings.

OLIVER: And do you...do you enjoy your work?

ALAN: Used to be a chef. In the Royal Navy.

34

OLIVER: Oh and was that...

ALAN: Best days of me life.

OLIVER: I've always been something of a landlubber myself so...

ALAN: A good aircraft carrier: one of the wonders of the modern world.

OLIVER: Yes, well, I did spend a good many years at the Ministry of Defence so...

ALAN: Like a great floating city.

OLIVER: So I do have a basic understanding of...

ALAN: Like one big happy family.

OLIVER: It was just communications essentially but I did...

ALAN: One of your kids knock these out then?

OLIVER: I beg your pardon?

ALAN: See, when you're in the armed forces you feel this real sense of purpose, you know, all your mates together, everyone knowing their place, their function, everyone looking out for one another. There's a real sense of happiness, you don't have to think about anything else, you just get up in the mornings and you know what you have to do with your day, it's all mapped out for you, structured, like being at school sort of thing and you know you're just a small cog in a great machine, but a machine that's serving a real good purpose and so you have no real worries. Not like now, not like being a postie. A postie just posts letters. He's not fighting for freedom or protecting his country, he's just putting letters through your letterbox and, as I say, worrying about his bills and his mortgage and whether or not he'll ever see his wife bloody smile again and...

OLIVER: I suppose just having any sort of employment at this moment in history is something to...

ALAN: A postman's just another boring job, right?

OLIVER: Well, you are of course performing a useful public service so…

ALAN: I reckon all men need a bit of danger in their lives.

OLIVER: I'm currently trying to work out what the hell I want to do with rest of my…

ALAN: We all need to feel as we're risking something.

OLIVER: Workwise, I mean,

ALAN: We all need to feel we're out there, fighting.

OLIVER: I'm sure I wasn't born to rewrite all this turgid governmental copy day after day…

ALAN: So when we do bring home the bacon each night it's as if we've achieved something, risked something.

OLIVER: Uploading files and downloading files and…

ALAN: It's how we get our sense of self-respect.

OLIVER: I mean, I did think I had more to offer the world than just…

ALAN: Like prehistoric man. He'd have to go out for days at a time, hunting these beasts, sometimes risking his own life. For the sake of his wife, for the sake of his kiddies.

OLIVER: More than just…well, what I'm currently…

ALAN: And when he came back with his kill he'd share out the meat with the whole community. Everyone, no matter who, would get exactly the same amount.

OLIVER: Emily would approve of that, of course.

ALAN: You know something: we could have got bombed or torpedoed at any time, day or night.

OLIVER: That seems to be the essence of her socialism.

ALAN: *(Taking money from his wallet.)* Mate, I'll give you twenty quid right now if you can guess what me official title were. Because me official title weren't 'chef' at all of course. It were…

OLIVER: Well, you see I do know this.

ALAN: You'll never guess it.

OLIVER: What I'm saying is I know because it's part of my job to…

ALAN: Never in a million years will you.

OLIVER: But I do know the answer, Alan.

ALAN: Go on, have a stab at it!

OLIVER: It's Catering Services Logistician.

ALAN amazed.

As I was saying, I have spent many years working at the MoD so…

ALAN: Nobody has ever, ever, ever, ever guessed that right before!

ALAN presses the banknote into OLIVER's hand.

OLIVER: Seriously, I'm not accepting this.

ALAN: Fair's fair!

OLIVER: Please.

ALAN: You guessed it correctly. Therefore you get the prize and that's the end of it!

ALAN opens another can. They fall into silence.

Got a bit of a drink problem as it happens.

OLIVER: Listen…

ALAN: And the problem is: I just can't get enough of the stuff!

He laughs wildly. The laugh dies away.

They do not speak for a time.

OLIVER: I'm really not going to take this money.

ALAN: I did a bit of stand-up too, as it goes. When I were younger.

OLIVER: *(Holding out the note.)* So please…

ALAN: Did a few of the pubs and clubs, you know.

OLIVER: I really must insist.

ALAN: *(Walking away, looking around.)* Used to really make people laugh. Used to really make people... I dunno... happy.

OLIVER: I'll just put it here then.

ALAN: Because that's what it's all about. Whatever you do in life you need to ask yourself. 'Does this or does this not make people happy?'

OLIVER: *(Putting the note on the table.)* Your money's just here.

ALAN: They built a statue to the great Bill Shankly, manager of Liverpool Football Club. And under this statue are written the words: HE MADE THE PEOPLE HAPPY.

OLIVER: Not really a football man so...

ALAN: Took them from a bog-standard second division side to become masters of the known universe.

OLIVER: Good for him.

ALAN: If on your deathbed you can look back on your life and you can in all honesty say you've done just that, well...

They do not speak. ALAN looks around.

You know what? I reckon you and me could become good mates. Don't see much of me mates these days to be fair. Some have moved away. Others aren't allowed out that often. We're all sort of slowly...drifting apart.

OLIVER: So like your wife were you born in this part of the...?

ALAN: Interesting paintings.

OLIVER: They're Em's actually.

ALAN: What, you mean they're not by a kiddie?

OLIVER: Her style has been likened to that of Jackson Pollock.

ALAN: Jackson Bollock, eh!?

ALAN laughs wildly. OLIVER smiles politely. The laugh dies away. They stand in silence for a time.

Some'at of an artist meself as it goes.

OLIVER: Oh really?

ALAN: Portraits mainly.

OLIVER: I see.

ALAN: Of me cat mainly.

OLIVER: That's…nice.

ALAN: A few of Dawn too.

OLIVER: Oh yes?

ALAN: With her kit off.

OLIVER: Oh, lovely.

ALAN: To be honest, pal, she is a total work of art herself. You know, in the nudity department. You can imagine. When we were younger… Everyone were after her and she chose me for some reason…and when we first, I tell people this and they… What I mean is, when we first, you know, between you and me, when she first removed her clobber, like, you know what I did?

OLIVER: No?

ALAN: I only went and burst into tears, didn't I!

OLIVER: That is…well…

ALAN: I was just so in love with her, Oliver, and I never in a million years thought a beautiful girl like her would ever… you know.

A silence.

But nowadays she's… You know, if I can be…? You see, these days, for quite a few years now really… I mean, we don't ever seem to ever… You know.

EMILY and DAWN on.

EMILY: …and as well as the banking system, all housing stock should be nationalised, it should all be communally owned and then rents could be set, which are fair and affordable and then that money should be used to maintain the said housing stock and to help improve communities. Look at young people starting out now, it's a nightmare: they're in debt up to their eyeballs, having had to pay for their

39

education, an education which was incidentally free for these privileged, middle-class people who implemented the student loan system, and then there are no jobs for them of course and if they're foolish enough to want to own their own home and start a family then heaven help them...

DAWN: As I say, we rely on our credit cards to...

EMILY: Housing, healthcare, education, our public utilities, public transport, these things should all be owned *by* and exist *for* the people.

DAWN: Mate of mine at work says we oughta rename the country 'Tescoland'.

EMILY: We are all of us now just the slaves of the banks and the corporations!

ALAN: But that new Tesco's is great, intit?

OLIVER: We don't tend to use supermarkets.

EMILY: That's because they destroy local communities.

ALAN: Do they?

EMILY: And community is everything.

ALAN: Well, I agree with that.

EMILY: Look at how our ancestors lived. Organically, sustainably, living as part of nature, living communally, not cut off and isolated from each other in these lonely little couples...

OLIVER: We're not that lonely, are we?

EMILY: Everything was shared. There was no ownership. There were no husbands or wives. Children were raised by the collective. You didn't say "This is *my* child or this is *my* wife or this is *my* house." The words ME and MY and MINE were just about non-existent.

DAWN: What, so you mean free love?

EMILY: All I'm saying is that the way we live today...it's all gone horribly wrong somewhere along the line.

They do not speak for a time.

40

OLIVER: Anchovy, anyone?

ALAN/DAWN: Not for me.

They do not speak for a time.

OLIVER: You'd absolutely hate to live in a commune.

EMILY: No, I wouldn't.

OLIVER: You don't like other people.

EMILY: Here I am inviting other people into my home, am I not?

OLIVER: What I mean is…

EMILY: So of course I *like* other people.

OLIVER: What I mean is you're not someone who generally…

EMILY: No idea what he's talking about.

She smiles at her guests.

They do not speak for a time. Awkward.

OLIVER: Alan here was just admiring your artwork.

EMILY: Nothing, Dawn, shall go well in England until all things are held in common.

OLIVER: He's a keen painter himself.

DAWN gives her husband a stern look.

ALAN: Just making conversation.

OLIVER: And you pose naked for him, I hear?

DAWN: I do bloody not!

ALAN: I paint her from memory.

DAWN: He mainly paints that daft old cat.

EMILY: Seems no one's listening to me so…

ALAN: Wondered if I could show you? Could do with the opinion of an expert.

DAWN: If you bring any of me over, I swear to God…

ALAN: I'll only bring the ones of Vince, I'll only bring a couple of the cat…

ALAN rushes off.

DAWN: What kind of man names his pet after an aircraft carrier?

OLIVER: Vince is…?

DAWN: HMS Invincible.

A long, awkward silence.

EMILY: So I might as well go and check on the baby.

EMILY heads for the stairs.

DAWN and OLIVER stare at each other.

OLIVER: She's two and a half actually. She's hardly a…she's hardly a baby.

DAWN and OLIVER in awkward silence.

Might I possibly interest you in a salted cashew nut?

DAWN: You know some'at: I reckon you're a bit of a dark horse, you.

OLIVER: How do you mean, sorry?

DAWN: Oh, I think you know exactly what I mean, posh boy.

She drinks, smiles, while OLIVER coughs nervously.

SCENE 5

EMILY is holding up a large framed painting of a cat and examining it. Nobody speaks for a time.

ALAN: Suspense is killing me.

She continues to look at the painting.

I've got a better one just here. But me best one be far is of Dawn lying stark bollock naked on our sofa but she won't ever let me show that to anyone.

DAWN: Too right I won't…

ALAN: Feel proper nervous.

EMILY continues to look at the painting.

42

OLIVER: Are you going to be delivering your verdict any time soon or…?

ALAN: Never had anyone who knows about art take a look before. But I want you to be honest. I want you to say if you think I've got any ability.

OLIVER: Well, in my humble opinion, I think it's got a certain amount of…

ALAN: Because my sister-in-law, that's my brother's wife, she's a bright woman, she's actually a librarian and *she* thinks I could make money out of them. She reckons people'd pay me to paint portraits of their kids or their cats or their whatever. But I'm a bit shy, you know, I don't know if I'm good enough to charge, so if *you* reckon that I could, well… I'd really value your opinion.

EMILY: Well, what can I say…

ALAN: Because it's when I'm at me happiest, you know, when I'm up in me room, with me little apron on and I just sort of let rip, let me imagination run wild and of course when I'm painting Vince I have to work off a photo because it's not always easy to get a cat to sit still for you for an hour so's you can get his eyes or his whiskers or his tail just right. *(He laughs.)* I did go to evening classes for a time but the woman there kept making us paint all this bastard fruit. Every week it were more fruit in these daft wooden bowls. One week it were bananas, another week it were apples, then it might be grapes or strawberries or oranges or…

DAWN: We get the idea, thank you.

ALAN: You get the idea.

DAWN: I think we do.

ALAN: And one time they brought us in this life model but she were bigger than the back end of a bus!

ALAN laughs. It dies away.

EMILY continues to look at the painting.

My art teacher always said I had potential and so I sort of kept it up, you know, and when I were at sea I drew sketches of a lot of me mates so they could send stuff back home to their wives and girlfriends and as I say…

DAWN: Do *you* sell any of your paintings then?

EMILY: It has been known, yes.

DAWN: You get much for them?

EMILY: That one there is *The Reunification of the Body and the Soul in a Time of Grieving.*

DAWN: And so what would someone pay you for it?

OLIVER: She's been offered just over a thousand for that.

DAWN: You're taking the piss, right?

EMILY: Excuse me?

DAWN: A thousand pound?!

EMILY: But I wouldn't part with it if I was offered ten times that amount.

OLIVER: But we need all the money we can get, don't we?

EMILY: I am never under any circumstances whatsoever selling that painting, Oliver!

An awkward silence.

I actually intend to start up a group for local artists and we're going to look into maybe doing up an old building and turning it into a gallery.

OLIVER: So that what you term 'real people' can show off the fruits of their labours. To encourage everyone to find the creativity that's within every…

ALAN: That'd be great!

OLIVER: It's about the democratisation of…

ALAN: Imagine that, love?

DAWN: I'm trying.

EMILY continues to look at the painting. They all look to her.

44

EMILY: Well, Alan…what can I say?

ALAN: Well, what *can* you say?

OLIVER: Well, *I* think it's got a certain something.

ALAN: Do you?

OLIVER: I think it has a certain, and please don't take this the wrong way, a certain insouciance about it which, frankly, I find rather refreshing.

ALAN: Refreshing?

OLIVER: A sort of carefree style which is unencumbered by any… What I mean to say is, Alan, your untutored eye lends these paintings a quality which is…

DAWN: But what does *she* think?

ALAN: Yes, what does *she* think?

DAWN: Because *she's* the professional.

EMILY: I really don't know what to say.

ALAN: It's that good, is it?

He laughs. The laugh fades. He picks up the other framed painting.

This one's a bit better than that one. I call it *Vince Staring Out The Window.*

EMILY: So what's this one?

ALAN: *Vince With A Rat in His Mouth.*

OLIVER: I think you capture that very well.

ALAN: Ta very much…

EMILY puts the painting down.

EMILY: Well, I have to say: I do quite admire the frames.

ALAN: The frames?

EMILY: I can see that you've framed them yourself and I'd say you've done rather a good job.

ALAN: Me dad were a joiner so…

EMILY: Yes, I can see you've got some skill.

ALAN: I fitted our kitchen.

DAWN: Though it's always falling apart.

EMILY: Well, as I say, you've done a really, really good job.

ALAN: Can't do it for too long though as it does me back in.

DAWN: You need to lose some weight.

ALAN: It's a trapped nerve.

They do not speak.

DAWN: Go on then, what about the cats?

EMILY: Well, Alan, you said you wanted me to be honest?

ALAN: I do. I want you to tell me the truth.

EMILY: The brutal truth?

OLIVER: Not too brutal, I hope.

ALAN: The brutal truth, yeah.

EMILY: Well, I'm afraid to say, that in my humble opinion, your paintings are not terribly good.

DAWN laughs and then a silence descends.

ALAN: What, neither of them?

EMILY: I'm afraid not.

Nobody speaks.

ALAN: What, I mean…are you sure?

EMILY: Quite sure.

OLIVER: Oh, Em, come on…

EMILY: What?

ALAN: I could always get the one of Dawn.

DAWN: You could not!

EMILY: It's okay, I think I've seen enough.

OLIVER: Would anyone care for another olive?

ALAN: So, what, you don't think I could sell them?

EMILY: Well, if you can manage to find someone who's willing to part with their hard-earned…

ALAN: You don't think I've got any talent at all?

EMILY: I really don't want to hurt your feelings.

ALAN: *Other* folk have said they liked them.

EMILY: Well, that's great then…

ALAN: Because you could be wrong?

EMILY: Of course I could be.

ALAN: Other folk have said they'd like me to paint their portrait.

EMILY: Then that's wonderful…

ALAN: But you'd say I'm just wasting me time?

EMILY: The important thing is to paint for yourself.

ALAN: I do.

EMILY: So it's something you do for your own pleasure. If other people happen to like what you've produced then so much the better.

ALAN: But that one there *has* given other people pleasure. They've said.

EMILY: So ignore me then…

ALAN: Mick said, Fat Judy said.

EMILY: As I say, Alan, feel free to ignore my opinion.

ALAN: Aunty May said she absolutely loved it, din't she? One hundred and ten per cent. Said she wanted me to do one of her Goldie.

DAWN: That's her guide dog.

EMILY: Aunty May is blind, is she?

ALAN: Only partially.

EMILY now bursts out laughing and is unable to control herself.

Think we'd better go.

OLIVER: Please don't leave with any bad feelings or…

EMILY: I'm sorry, honestly.

DAWN: If it makes you feel any better: I much prefer *your* paintings to hers.

ALAN: Do you?

DAWN: Thousand pound or no thousand pound.

EMILY: You are of course joking?

DAWN: Don't do owt for me.

EMILY: Well, I'm sorry about that.

DAWN: Looks like you've just thrown a load of different paints over the canvas and then messed about with it with your fingers.

OLIVER: Well, that is in effect what she does do.

EMILY: I beg your pardon?

OLIVER: Broadly speaking.

EMILY: That is not 'broadly speaking' what I do, thank you very much.

DAWN: At least *his* are of something.

EMILY: Are they indeed?

ALAN: I really thought this one were good.

EMILY: Well, I'm sorry to disabuse you of...

ALAN: I put hours and hours into it.

DAWN: At least we can see it's a cat.

EMILY: Well, to be honest, if he hadn't already told me it was a painting of his cat I might have been hard pressed to identify exactly what kind of creature it's supposed to represent.

ALAN: It's clearly a cat!

EMILY: Looks more like a boss-eyed hedgehog to me.

OLIVER: Em, come on!

EMILY: Well, it does.

DAWN: At least he's trying to paint something that actually exists.

EMILY: Art, my dear girl, is about feeling and emotion. It's about expressing the inexpressible. What's inside you, the feelings inside you, the sadness, the happiness, the anger, the love, the grief, it's about all these things finding some kind of external…

ALAN: Emily, that is exactly how I feel when I paint!

EMILY: But I'm afraid it doesn't translate.

ALAN: It does!

EMILY: I'm sorry but it doesn't.

ALAN: It really does!

EMILY: It simply does not!

ALAN: It's only when I paint I don't feel so lonely!

EMILY: Well, that simply doesn't translate onto your painting.

ALAN: It does, it does!

OLIVER: Let's not all fall out about this. I think we can all agree that Alan *does* have some talent and that his paintings *are*…

EMILY: No! No! This is exactly what's… God, it makes me want to tear my hair out to hear you say that! We have to tell the truth! We can't go through life being fake, fake, fake all the time! He asked me for my opinion and I gave it. That is the truth. He should be adult enough to accept that. He has no talent at all but if it gives him pleasure to paint then of course it's perfectly fine. But if you put something in front of an audience and you ask for an opinion then, yes, man up and take that opinion. What's the point in lying like this? *You* know he can't paint, *I* know he can't paint and probably deep down somewhere even *he* knows he can't paint. We always have to tell the truth in this life! We have to be honest! Look at us, we've just been making polite, banal conversation all evening! Nobody wants to talk about what actually matters: that big business is going out of its way to make money from the wholesale destruction of the planet, that Western powers behave like psychopaths, forever sending misguided, ignorant soldiers off to murder innocent civilians in illegal wars! That every single day the Palestinians are suffering the most appalling…

ALAN: Hold on a minute, love!

EMILY: I will not hold on!

ALAN: Ignorant, did you say?

EMILY: And I am not your 'love'!

DAWN: People out there are laying down their lives for you!

ALAN: So you shouldn't disrespect them.

EMILY: I am not disrespecting anybody!

DAWN: Every day our boys are dying for you!

EMILY: I never asked them to!

ALAN: Defending you and your family from those evil…

EMILY: But we are not under attack from anybody!

DAWN: What about them planes hitting them towers? What about them bombers on the Tube?!

ALAN: Makes me really upset when I hear that kind of talk…

OLIVER: I think what Emily means is…

EMILY: Emily is perfectly capable of explaining what Emily means…

ALAN: You've no idea how brave these people are…

EMILY: Their bravery is not in question…

ALAN: Lives have been destroyed.

EMILY: But you only care about *British* lives!

ALAN: I'm British and I'm proud!

EMILY: And you just assume, you don't even think about it, you just blindly assume that we are always, always the good guys!

DAWN: Of course we're the good guys!

ALAN: They're dying for you, for me, for freedom, for the love of this great country!

EMILY: *Au contraire*, Alan. They are being sacrificed at the altar of imperialism, for the sake of oil merchants and arms dealers and to help line the pockets of...

DAWN: So would you rather be a woman in this country or would you...

EMILY: That's just not the point!

DAWN: Or would you prefer to live like a dog under the Taliban?

EMILY: If you'll only listen to me then you might just learn something!

DAWN: Those men are just savages!

EMILY: I am, thank you, perfectly aware of the moral shortcomings of...

ALAN: Now, you listen to me, okay! Me and her: we've got a son, a wonderful son who's out there right now! A twenty-year-old lad who's risking his life so's you can be free to paint your pictures and eat your olives and have all your clever opinions! He's twenty years old and he's a national hero! They all are! Every last one of them, dead or alive! National heroes!

ALAN picks up his paintings. He storms out. A silence descends.

OLIVER: Dawn, honestly...

DAWN: You might, love, want to have a quiet little think about that.

She follows her husband out. Stunned, EMILY watches her go as OLIVER, almost without thinking, pockets ALAN's banknote.

Act Two

A few weeks later. EMILY, open-mouthed, and OLIVER. He has just made a shocking announcement.

EMILY: You have *got* to be joking?

OLIVER: I just think it's important.

EMILY: But we've *talked* about this for years and we…

OLIVER: I know we have but what you fail to…

EMILY: I cannot *believe* you'd do something like that.

OLIVER: Well, I'm sorry.

EMILY: After everything we've…

OLIVER: I just think that now's the time.

EMILY: It's not worthy of you.

OLIVER: Oh, come on…

EMILY: I feel gutted, to be honest.

OLIVER: It's just something I feel I…

EMILY: I feel completely…betrayed.

OLIVER: Aren't you being a bit…

EMILY: You have *seriously* re-joined the Labour Party?!

He does not respond.

The same Labour Party we have spent the last fifteen…

OLIVER: I'm just tired of feeling so…

EMILY: …the last fifteen years despairing about!

OLIVER: …disaffected.

EMILY: 'Government is merely the shadow cast by big business over society.'

OLIVER: Comrade Chomsky, I presume?

EMILY: Merely participating in this fraudulent system is…

OLIVER: But I am not an anarchist…

EMILY: It's not a question of anarchy!

OLIVER: We've got to get the right wing out, surely?

EMILY: But they are *all* right wing!

OLIVER: Okay, but…

EMILY: They stopped representing working people twenty, thirty years ago…

OLIVER: At least when New Labour came in there was some kind of…

EMILY: Oliver, we replaced the Tories with a lying, murdering…

OLIVER: I knew you wouldn't approve so…

EMILY: Whatever moral authority the Labour Party ever had went up in smoke the day they buried John Smith.

OLIVER: Isn't that something of a mixed metaphor?

EMILY: John Smith was a man of…

OLIVER: Yes, but he was in opposition so…

EMILY: He was a man of integrity…

OLIVER: But he was hardly a socialist…

EMILY: He was no Tony Benn but at least…

OLIVER: He was just a lawyer with conservative values…

EMILY: Well, he wasn't Blair. He wasn't some power-crazed, warmongering…

OLIVER: And Tony Benn has been proved wrong about almost everything!

EMILY: How can you say that!?

OLIVER: For God's sake, Emily, he happily confessed to admiring Chairman Mao!

EMILY: What he said actually said was…

OLIVER: And Marx advocated violence so…

EMILY: You're just another…fearful liberal, Oliver. And the liberal class has been seduced by wealth and by security…

OLIVER: It's easy to have integrity when you have no power.

EMILY: New Labour destroyed everything real, decent people believed in. They took away the voice of the ordinary citizen forever…

OLIVER: Like your friend Mr Benn you do have this tendency to sentimentalise the working classes…

EMILY: And now the corporations will rule for God knows how long and…

OLIVER: Oh, the corporations, the corporations…

EMILY: All these faceless careerists who'll do or say anything simply to get…

OLIVER: We have to make the most of who we've got and hope…

EMILY: We need to bring about radical change to the way…

OLIVER: Well, if I can be frank…

EMILY: There's no real democracy and you know it. There's no actual choice!

OLIVER: If I can be frank with you…

EMILY: Oh, feel free to be frank.

OLIVER: You and your group of nice middle-class ladies with their nice middle-class clothing and their nice middle-class haircuts, all of you standing about in the high street handing out all your leaflets…

EMILY: So, you're deriding my campaigning?

OLIVER: I'm not deriding anything. I'm just…

EMILY: And the urgency to act on climate change is being completely ignored…

OLIVER: We know, we know…

EMILY: Where are the writers, the broadcasters, the TV personalities, where are the brave ones screaming: 'No, sorry! Capitalism is not this invincible, unassailable engine of human progress!'? I'll tell you...

OLIVER: We need to assimilate the Green movement and the Anti-war movement into…

EMILY: Mainstream politics?

OLIVER: Of course.

EMILY: But if anyone ever stood up in mainstream politics and called for Blair to stand trial as a war criminal they'd just be ridiculed…

OLIVER: I agree but that's…

EMILY: *(Tearful.)* That man must one day be held accountable!

OLIVER: We have to work with the world as it is.

EMILY: And now he's travelling around, lecturing about peace, making his millions…

OLIVER: And stop trying to be perfect all the time.

EMILY: When he should be spending the rest of his life in some tiny prison cell weeping and rocking and…

OLIVER: I don't want to antagonise you but…

EMILY: Makes me sick to the stomach…

OLIVER: Emily…

EMILY: I so hate him, Oliver! I just so hate that revolting man. And I hate the fact he makes me hate so much because I want to love, I so want to feel love…

OLIVER: It's just the way of the world.

EMILY: Oh, the way of the world…

OLIVER: The way of the world, yes.

EMILY: And last week it was Facebook, Oliver! A man your age joining Facebook!

OLIVER: I just want to feel more…

EMILY: Why do people have this terror…

OLIVER: …connected.

EMILY: …this absolute terror of being anonymous?

OLIVER: *(Shouting.)* I've just been feeling lonely, okay!

They do not speak for a time.

EMILY: Well, I'm sure your mother will be very proud.

OLIVER: What's that supposed to be mean?

EMILY: Isn't she still an ardent supporter of the Labour Party?

OLIVER: At the moment she has other rather more pressing things on her…

EMILY: Since she finally abandoned her devotion to Thatcher.

OLIVER: I'm not joining for her.

EMILY: Because she thought Blair had, and I quote, 'a jolly nice smile'?

OLIVER: You really need to work on your impersonation of Mum because…

EMILY: And, yes, what a brilliant job they did attracting all those *Daily Mail* fascists to the party…

OLIVER: My mother is not a fascist.

EMILY: Almost every sentence she utters starts with the words: 'You mustn't think me racist but…'

OLIVER: You make her sound like a drunk Queen Victoria or…

EMILY: The woman still has servants, for God's sake…

OLIVER: She has a cleaner and a gardener but so do lots of…

EMILY: I just knew when people like her started voting Labour the writing was on the wall for…

OLIVER: Listen, she'll be dead in a few months, won't she, so that'll be one less fascist for you to worry about.

A silence.

EMILY: What a horrible thing to say.

OLIVER: I'm sorry. I'm just…

EMILY: What a horrible, horrible thing to say.

They do not speak for a time.

OLIVER: It's been a stressful week. What say we…what say we crack open a bottle of wine?

Appalled, she stares at him.

EMILY: You are not serious?

OLIVER: Em, we are not alcoholics. We never were alcoholics. We were very drunk that night and what happened happened but it wasn't…

EMILY: If we hadn't been so drunk then…

OLIVER: How many times do we have to have this…?

EMILY: He was dying alone in his cot while we were both…

OLIVER: There was nothing we could have…

EMILY: …both dancing like lunatics to some of your ridiculous…funk!

OLIVER: …there is nothing at all we could have done!

They do not speak for a time. He puts his hand on her shoulder.

We really need to start being happy again.

EMILY: I don't care about being happy anymore. I just want to be at peace.

OLIVER: You are a good and decent person so…

EMILY: And these terrible thoughts in my head all the time: why are *her* derivative paintings more respected than mine, why does *he* make more money than me, why does *my* child have to die and not *hers*? Why not her ugly, fat, screeching brat instead of my beautiful little…

OLIVER: Let's just, tonight…

EMILY: And these are clearly not the thoughts of a decent person, are they?

OLIVER: …after four years of self-flagellation…let's please, just once at least, let's please try to have a little bit of fun.

She does not respond. He goes to the kitchen area. Locates a secreted bottle of wine. Two glasses. Returns. She watches him. He waits for her approval. Gets nothing. Opens the bottle. He pours a glass. Is about to pour another. She puts her hand over it. He puts the bottle down. He slowly and rather nervously brings his glass to his lips. She watches him.

Am I going to burn in hell?

EMILY: Possibly.

OLIVER: Well, I wasn't raised by Puritans so I don't have to…

EMILY: My parents are *Quakers*, Oliver! Not Puritans!

He pours wine into the second glass.

This is a pretty serious moment, isn't it? We made a vow that we would never again under any circumstances…

OLIVER: It's been so deadly serious for so long. Please. I just want us to have a little bit of…a little bit of pleasure.

EMILY: You do what you have to do, Oliver.

He drinks. She watches him. She turns away. Gathers herself. They do not speak.

OLIVER: Please, come and have a drink.

EMILY: *(Back to him, upset.)* You haven't seen that wretched cat on your travels, have you?

OLIVER: What cat?

EMILY: Next door's cat? Vincent or whatever they call it?

He does not reply.

Their girls called round this afternoon. Megan. Sophie. While you were out running. Very charming actually. Both in a real state about it. It's been missing for almost a week apparently. They've been posting these leaflets all over town. They're offering a hundred pounds reward, it seems. The younger one was absolutely inconsolable. Broke down on the doorstep. I didn't know what to say. It was rather touching. Very polite and very pleasant girls. I hesitate to say they are a credit to their parents. And let's hope it's us who spot the thing. We could do with the money.

OLIVER drinks.

OLIVER: This wine is top dollar.

EMILY: Oliver, you know how much I loathe that expression.

OLIVER: Sorry.

He pours another glass, drinks. She watches him for a time.

Well, the sad fact of the matter is that…their cat is dead.

EMILY: Their cat is dead?

OLIVER: Their cat is dead, yes.

EMILY: What do you mean, dead?

OLIVER: What do I mean by 'dead'?

EMILY: What do you mean by 'dead', yes.

OLIVER: I mean dead as in dead. The cat is dead.

She stares at him.

EMILY: That's wonderful then.

OLIVER: Is it?

EMILY: Isn't it?

He drinks some more.

How do you know?

OLIVER: I know because I killed it.

She looks at him in horror.

EMILY: You killed it?

OLIVER: I'm afraid I did.

EMILY: How do you mean, you killed it?

OLIVER: I mean that I terminated its earthly existence…

EMILY: I mean, *why* did…?

OLIVER: I didn't mean to.

EMILY: Oh my God.

OLIVER: I was doing some weeding and I saw it sitting on the guinea pig run, just crouching there, eyeing them up. I shouted at it, clapped my hands at it, but it just turned and stared at me, with this arrogant, imperious look. So

I picked up this stone, this rather large stone, and I just lobbed it. Without thinking really. Must have been thirty yards away.

EMILY: And you hit it?

OLIVER slaps his forehead with the palm of his hand. He drinks.

OLIVER: Then I went over to it and, well, it was just about alive, breathing weakly, but its skull was all caved in.

EMILY: Jesus, Oliver...

OLIVER: So I fetched the spade and finished it off.

EMILY: I feel sick.

OLIVER: And then I buried it just there. Where it was lying. Just there by the apple tree.

EMILY: Did anyone see you?

OLIVER shrugs. EMILY thinks hard. Now she eyes the other glass of wine. She looks at it with an uncertain eye. Slowly she brings the glass to her lips. Smells it. She drinks. They both drink.

SCENE 2

Several hours later. James Brown's 'Get Up (I Feel Like Being a) Sex Machine' is in its last ninety seconds or so. A wine bottle now stands half-empty. Another two stand empty beside it. OLIVER and EMILY dancing (terribly, embarrassingly) around the coffee table. One on the air guitar, the other the air piano. They are both miming the words perfectly: a long-remembered, well-rehearsed routine. Drunk (EMILY very much so), they finally stop dancing as the song ends with its five chords.

EMILY: I should like, sir, to propose a toast!

OLIVER: Please do, madam.

EMILY: To Vince!

OLIVER: To Vince!

EMILY: To Vince!

OLIVER: Let us indeed drink to poor, dear Vince!

EMILY: To the regrettable demise of that murderous, that murderous…

OLIVER: To Vince!

EMILY: To Vince!

BOTH: We will remember him!

They laugh wildly.

EMILY: May he rest in peace!

OLIVER: May he rest in peace beneath our apple tree!

EMILY: Beneath the sod!

OLIVER: And let our children's guinea pigs, let our children's guinea pigs…whatever their names are… Let them all sleep soundly in their beds…

EMILY: Cages!

OLIVER: Their cages, yes!

EMILY: And so let me be quite clear about this…

OLIVER: Quite clear!

EMILY: We were not prepared to simply stand back…

OLIVER: Simply stand back!

EMILY: And allow those innocent rodents…

OLIVER: We were not going to be appeasers, no!

EMILY: To allow those innocent rodents to live in terror…

OLIVER: To live in terror under the tyranny of this violent, this cruel…

EMILY: This despicable…

OLIVER: This abominable…

BOTH: Vince!

EMILY: Ding-dong the Vince is dead!

OLIVER: Which old Vince?

EMILY: The wicked Vince!

BOTH: Ding-dong the Wicked Vince is dead!

EMILY pours them more wine.

EMILY: I have to say… I have to say that I find it rather odd…odd that you…that you are drinking from this glass because I always understood, I always understood that you were… *(As ALAN.)* …an Out the Can Man.

OLIVER: *(Also as ALAN.)* I says, d'you think me paintings are any good, like? I mean, d'you think I've got any ability?

EMILY: *(As DAWN.)* Well, I'll tell you some'at for nowt, mate: they're a bugger sight better than that snooty old bitch's next door.

OLIVER: I got a new one, you know.

EMILY: Oh yeah? What's it called?

OLIVER: This one's called *Vince Lying on the Grass Wi' His Brains Bashed In.*

EMILY: Ee, that's bloody brilliant, pal!!

OLIVER: And this one here's called *Vince Six Feet Under and Riddled Wi' Worms.*

EMILY: Ee, it's a ruddy masterpiece, is that!

OLIVER: You think so, pal?

EMILY: One hundred and ten per cent!

They fall about laughing once more.

After a time EMILY seems to sober up and her laughter dies away. OLIVER's continues. Then he notices her change of mood.

OLIVER: What?

EMILY: I thought I heard the baby.

OLIVER: She's fast asleep.

EMILY: Will you please, please check on her?

OLIVER: No, I won't!

EMILY: Then *I* will check on her…

OLIVER: No, you won't…

He grabs her arm to stop her leaving.

EMILY: What are you doing?

OLIVER: Just stay here.

EMILY: This is all wrong.

OLIVER: There's nothing wrong.

He sits her down. She is becoming maudlin through the drink.

EMILY: There's something decidedly wrong with me.

OLIVER: There is *nothing* wrong with…

EMILY: I'm never at peace with the present moment. I need to make friends with the present moment. I…

OLIVER: Emily, please…

EMILY: I have such nightmares.

OLIVER: I know, I know…

EMILY: The ruined world our children will grow up in… Ten billion people… And the slaughter that's coming will make those terrible wars seem like…a child's tea party… And what's worse: they're going to have to do jobs! They're both going to have to do boring, boring jobs! Shouldn't have had children. Why did we? Why? Selfish, so selfish…

She stands and sways.

Our children are going to suffer, Oliver. They are going to pay for our crimes.

OLIVER: You do seem extremely drunk…

EMILY: I want Alfie back. I want you to bring him back to me. Miss my boy. Feel so guilty. Every minute of every day!

He goes to her.

He was so cold, Oliver. So cold, cold in my arms.

He comforts her.

(Swaying a little.) And the man looks at me with that pity in his eyes and says: 'I'm afraid, madam, this child is dead…' And my legs buckle and I'm crawling on the floor, trying not to be sick and this howl of pain, a sound that doesn't feel like it belongs to me, this animal howl coming from

63

somewhere inside me, this sound is linking me to the great universal pain of all the mothers, of all the mothers of all the ages, all the mothers who've ever howled over their dead children and...

She suddenly looks at him as if she's just remembered something important.

OLIVER: What is it?

EMILY: *(Swaying.)* You. Killed. Their. Cat.

OLIVER: It was an accident.

EMILY: And now we're just laughing about it!

OLIVER: We were only letting off a bit of...

EMILY: What's wrong with us?

OLIVER: I didn't mean to kill it.

EMILY: You threw a stone at it!

OLIVER: I only meant to scare it.

EMILY: What about those sweet girls?

OLIVER: They'll never know.

EMILY: But *we'll* know. Every single day for the rest of our lives we will know.

OLIVER: Emily...

EMILY: We'll know it's rotting away under our apple tree.

OLIVER: They'll probably just get another one.

EMILY: And will you kill that one too?

OLIVER: I thought you'd be pleased!

EMILY: So you killed it for me?

OLIVER: For you, for the kids and for the birds and guinea pigs.

EMILY: So you *did* mean to kill it?

OLIVER: It was thirty yards away. I just wanted to scare it away from the...

EMILY: We'll have to tell them!

64

OLIVER: Don't be ridiculous!

EMILY: I'm going to go round there right now and tell them what's happened.

OLIVER: Emily, please! Just calm down…

EMILY: I can see two of you!

OLIVER: We need to take a moment and…

EMILY: You need to tell them what you did!

OLIVER: He might attack me!

EMILY: We need to make friends with them!

OLIVER: We've already tried that and it didn't work!

EMILY: We've got to live next to them!

OLIVER: Emily, you're being…

EMILY: They're both good, decent, hardworking people!

OLIVER: We don't need to have anything to do with them. We can live next door to them and just smile politely at them whenever we see them. We don't need to have them as part of our lives.

EMILY: I want to know who my neighbours are. I want our kids to play with other kids in the street!

OLIVER: But nobody's kids play in the streets anymore!

EMILY: I want us to be able to leave our doors unlocked…

OLIVER: But that's just old-fashioned…

EMILY: I want us all to be able to drop in on each other and…

OLIVER: You'd hate that!

EMILY: I promised I'd never drink again!

OLIVER: I know you did but…

EMILY: You've got me drunk, Oliver!

OLIVER: Em, come on…

EMILY: They are genuine and decent people! Alan and Dawn. Dalan Dawn. Dalan Dawn.

He sits her down.

I am so...drunk.

OLIVER: It's okay. It's not a crime.

EMILY: It *is* a crime!

OLIVER: It's not!

They gather themselves for a time before she suddenly gets to her feet again.

EMILY: But we've simply got to tell them.

OLIVER: No!

EMILY: We've got to tell them about the cat!

OLIVER: Emily, please sit down!

EMILY: All we have in this life is the truth!

OLIVER: This will do us no good at all!

EMILY: Ordinary people! People way better than us!

OLIVER: I'm begging you...

EMILY: Must apologise! Must confess to Alan and Dawn! Good people, they're good people...

OLIVER: I beg you not to do this!

EMILY: And you and I, we are not fit to wipe the dirt, to wipe the dirt from off their feet.

OLIVER: Please, please don't do this!

EMILY: Must beg, beg, beg for forgiveness...

She staggers off.

He watches her as she leaves, unable to move for a time. And then hurries off after her.

SCENE 3

OLIVER alone, holding a wine glass.

OLIVER: *(To himself.)* Why do you always, always have to put me through this...

ALAN and DAWN now on.

…this kind of bollocks?

ALAN: Alright?

OLIVER: *(Turning.)* Hello there.

They do not speak for a time.

ALAN: You okay? You seem a bit…?

OLIVER: Fine, thank you…

He sways a little. They do not speak for a time.

DAWN: Hi there.

OLIVER: Hi.

They do not speak for a time.

Where's Emily?

ALAN: Outside. She seems a bit…

OLIVER: Does she?

ALAN: She said you had something you wanted to say to us.

OLIVER: Did she?

ALAN: Yeah.

They do not speak for a time.

OLIVER: It really is a super…super evening.

ALAN: Aye, it's not bad.

They do not speak for a time.

So?

OLIVER: So?

ALAN: She said it were important.

OLIVER: Did she?

They do not speak for a time.

ALAN: You going to tell us then?

OLIVER: Well…

ALAN: I don't wanna be rude, but…

OLIVER: Of course, no…

ALAN: But I don't really wanna stop here all night.

OLIVER: I understand.

ALAN: Just watched England lose on penalties so…

OLIVER: Oh, I am sorry…

ALAN: So I'm not in the best of moods…

OLIVER: They lost on penalties again?

ALAN: And, you know, I'm up at the crack of dawn so…

They do not speak for a time.

OLIVER: I'm sorry about…the loss.

ALAN: You what?

OLIVER: I mean, your loss. The loss. Your loss.

ALAN: You mean, England?

OLIVER: Yes.

ALAN: Every tournament, intit?

OLIVER: I quite understand.

ALAN: Sick joke it is. God or Fate or what you call it. Playing a sick joke on the English.

They do not speak for a time.

It's *our* sport. *We* invented it. We used to be top dogs. We used to rule the whole world.

OLIVER does not respond.

You sure you're alright? You seem a bit…

OLIVER: I'm afraid I'm just a little bit drunk.

ALAN: Thought you didn't drink?

OLIVER: I don't.

They do not speak for a time.

ALAN: So…?

OLIVER: This is about… Last week, well, unfortunately…what happened was…

ALAN: Oh, we can forget about all that!

OLIVER: Can we?

ALAN: We just got off on a bad footing. You know, arguing about my rubbish paintings and the war and…

OLIVER: No, it's not that. It's…

ALAN: And that night, pal… I made the decision: I'm never, ever picking up another paintbrush for as long as I live.

OLIVER: Oh, please don't say that!

ALAN: I went home and I smashed 'em all up.

OLIVER: Oh, Jesus, no…

ALAN: Sliced 'em all up with one of me Stanley knives…

OLIVER: You shouldn't have done that…

ALAN: Chopped up all the frames for firewood.

OLIVER: Oh, Alan, that's such a shame…

ALAN: Didn't I?

DAWN: You did.

ALAN: Just a big loser, that's me. Born wi' no talent. No talent whatsoever.

He laughs. They do not speak for a time.

Really thought we might just do it this time. Really thought we might scrape through to semis at least.

They do not speak for a time.

So… Not been a good week. Not been a good few weeks for me. Not been me usual self. Have I?

DAWN: You haven't.

OLIVER: I'm sorry to hear that.

ALAN: And I really miss my cat. I really miss him, you know.

They do not speak for a time. ALAN fighting back his upset.

Don't suppose he's been in your garden, has he?

OLIVER: Well…

ALAN: Me best mate is Vince.

OLIVER: I appreciate that.

ALAN: And it's not like him. To just run off. To miss his meals. He's never done this before.

They do not speak for a time.

Well, look. If that's all you wanted to say… Well, I'm sorry if I were a bit… And I know I can be. I tend to speak without thinking sometimes. Just open me gob and see what comes out. Usually it's a load of old rubbish. *(To DAWN.)* Intit? *(He laughs.)* So, you know. New neighbours and that. No hard feelings.

He extends a hand to OLIVER, who hesitates.

Let's just start again. We're different kinds of people and I accept that but there's no reason we can't all be friends. Is there?

OLIVER: Well, Alan. There probably is actually.

ALAN: Why's that then?

OLIVER: Because… Well, the truth is… What I need to say to you is rather more important than apologising for the other night. I really need to apologise to you for something else. Something I have done for which you may be quite unable to forgive me.

ALAN waits.

ALAN: Go on then, pal. You got me interest now.

OLIVER: Oh God… I don't know how… I don't quite know how to say this but…

DAWN: Then let *me* say it.

OLIVER: Let *you* say it?

DAWN: I'm the one what should tell him. *I'm* the one.

OLIVER: I'm not sure I follow, sorry.

ALAN: What's all this about?

Nobody speaks for a time.

70

OLIVER: Last week. One day last week… I'm really sorry to have to confess this to you but…

DAWN: Me and him did it.

OLIVER drops his wine glass. It smashes.

Nobody speaks for a time.

ALAN: You what?

DAWN: Me and him did it.

ALAN: You and him did it?

DAWN: Me and him did it, yeah.

Nobody speaks for a time.

ALAN: You and him did what?

DAWN: Me and him did *it*!

ALAN: It?

DAWN: It, Alan! It!

ALAN: You mean, you…?

DAWN: Had sex!

ALAN: Who with?

DAWN: With him!

ALAN: With him?

DAWN: We had sex with each other. Me and him.

ALAN: This one here?

DAWN: Him, look! The posh bloke standing just there wi' his gob wide open!

Nobody speaks for a time.

ALAN turns to OLIVER.

ALAN: Is this right, pal?

OLIVER does not respond, just blinks, gawps, swallows hards.

DAWN: Al, I'm so sorry.

ALAN: Jesus…

DAWN: But something needs to change.

ALAN sits down, his head in hands.

DAWN and OLIVER, dazed and confused, stare at each other.

OLIVER: Why. Did. You. Just.

DAWN: You what?

OLIVER: Why. Did. You.

DAWN: Better he hears it from me.

Nobody speaks. Then EMILY on.

OLIVER: Where have you been?

EMILY: Smoking a cigarette.

OLIVER: You gave up.

EMILY: Then swiftly resumed.

Nobody speaks.

So…you've confessed your crime?

DAWN: *I* told him.

EMILY: *You* told him?

DAWN: I told him, yeah.

EMILY: *(To OLIVER.)* Oh, you already told her, did you?

OLIVER: Listen…

EMILY: You told her before you told me?

OLIVER: I don't really…

EMILY: Alan, all I can say is: I'm desperately sorry this has happened. I mean, I realise I'm not the actual criminal here but…

ALAN: No, *he* is!

EMILY: But you have to understand that it was all quite by accident.

ALAN: How can a thing like that happen by accident?

EMILY: Well, he didn't mean it to happen.

OLIVER: Listen…

72

EMILY: Did you?

OLIVER: Well, no but…

EMILY: Is there perhaps some way we can make it up to you?

DAWN and ALAN stare at her.

I just want to be a good neighbour.

ALAN: Feel as if me life's over.

EMILY: There's no reason why we can't all remain adult and civilised about this unfortunate situation.

ALAN: Me heart's breaking here.

ALAN's head goes in his hands again.

EMILY: *(To DAWN.)* There must be something we can do?

DAWN: It takes two to tango, doesn't it?

EMILY: *(Confused.)* I suppose that's true but I'm not…

DAWN: So like you say let's just all be adults about it.

EMILY: Well, no, it's not the end of the world, is it? Of course obviously he's upset but…

DAWN: 'Nothing shall go well in England until all things are held in common.'

EMILY: Oh, very well said.

DAWN: And it's not as if we own each other, is it? The world doesn't stop spinning just because of something like this.

Not massively with it, EMILY sways.

You alright there?

EMILY: Can we offer him some form of…some form of remuneration? Can we not compensate you in some way?

ALAN: You can't compensate me for this!

EMILY: Alan, I quite understand but it is only a…

ALAN: I oughta rip his head off.

DAWN: Why don't you then?

EMILY: I'd really rather you didn't.

ALAN: You what?

DAWN: Not in your nature, is it?

EMILY: We believe in non-violence in this house.

ALAN: That what you want me to do, is it?

EMILY: I just don't want this to be something that…you know…means we can't…

DAWN: Some men are prepared to fight for what they believe in.

EMILY: …can't carry on being civil and pleasant towards each other.

They do not speak for a time.

DAWN: You know… I respect you.

EMILY: And I respect *you.*

DAWN: We respect each other.

EMILY: We do, we do…

DAWN: Because I *was* going to come round and apologise for…

EMILY: You mean for the other week?

DAWN: I don't normally behave like…

EMILY: Well, I suppose you *were* being a touch…

DAWN: But these things go on, right?

EMILY: These things go on, yes.

ALAN: Where then? Where did you do it?

DAWN: Why does that matter?

EMILY: Well, it was in our garden, wasn't it?

ALAN: In your garden?

EMILY: Just under the…just under the apple tree.

She sways some more. ALAN looks at OLIVER. And then at DAWN. Then his head in his hands again. EMILY staggers a little. OLIVER supports her.

74

ALAN seated, head still in hands. DAWN standing.

DAWN: Al.

ALAN: What?

DAWN: Let's just go home.

ALAN: You go.

DAWN: Please.

ALAN: I got no home now.

DAWN: Of course you've got a home.

> *ALAN begins to sob.*

We can't stop here all night.

ALAN: What made you do it?

DAWN: I don't know.

ALAN: You don't ever want to…you know…with me.

DAWN: No.

> *They do not speak for a time.*

ALAN: Have there been others?

DAWN: No!

ALAN: You swear?

DAWN: I swear to you.

> *They do not speak for a time.*

ALAN: Tell me something. Look me in the eye and tell me something straight: am I a boring person?

DAWN: I'm going home now.

ALAN: *Have* I become boring? *Am* I boring? Okay, I know I am. I know I bore you. I bore everyone. I *am* boring. I bore people. I talk too much and what I say is boring and I know most people I'm talking to probably think I'm really boring and last week I was talking to Fat Judy and you know how she can go on, how boring she can be, well, even *she* made me feel I was boring, I saw a sort of fixed smile on her face, a faraway look in her eyes and so, yes, when I look at folk sometimes, you know, especially folk that don't know me, when I'm talking to them I reckon they're thinking 'Jesus Christ, this man is possibly the most boring person I've ever come across in my entire life' and when I hear myself talking sometimes, when I'm sort of going on and on and on about something, I'm starting to think 'Jesus, Alan, shut up, will you, you really are becoming boring' but I can't always stop especially with a drink inside me and so I know I am, I know I have become quite boring these days, I've become a bore, you know, a boring person and so I just need to know on a scale of one to ten exactly how boring would you say I…

DAWN: For God's sake…

ALAN: I just need to…

DAWN: I don't know if *you're* boring or if *I'm* boring or…

ALAN: But do you love him? Are you in love with him?

DAWN: I don't know.

They do not speak.

ALAN: You know I've only ever been with you.

DAWN: We're just in this routine, Al. The same things every day.

ALAN: And that not very often.

DAWN: And we don't talk about anything…

ALAN: You know, I always knew I loved you more than you…

DAWN: …and life's just going by so quickly and…

ALAN: ….more than you loved me.

DAWN: …and sometimes I *can* feel sort of peaceful but…

ALAN: Always knew it.

DAWN: But most of the time I only feel half alive. I want to do something else. Be somewhere else.

ALAN: And I knew in my heart of hearts this would happen.

76

DAWN: It's like there's this great claw here that's pulling and tearing at my heart.

ALAN: Why can't we just be happy with the simple things?

DAWN: And I go from day to day like this machine. Tired, half-asleep.

ALAN: Just being together. Watching our girls grow up into these two beautiful young women.

DAWN: Like I'm just skimming the surface of things. Oliver reckons many people, well, they maybe settle too soon.

ALAN: You had a baby. I took you on.

DAWN: I'm so scared of the future.

ALAN: So what's he bloody talking about? What do these kind of people know?

They do not speak for a time.

Well, I know I can forgive you.

She says nothing.

I worship you, you know. To me you're like some…some goddess. And I do… I do forgive you.

DAWN: Why aren't you angry? Why aren't you… I don't know…throwing things about?

ALAN: I don't know.

DAWN: You know, you were more angry just now shouting at the England team.

ALAN: They were playing without heart. They were playing without pride.

DAWN: Jesus…

ALAN: Why didn't you ever talk to me? If you were feeling so…

DAWN: Because *you're* the one who talks. I'm the one who always has to…

ALAN: I'm listening *now*, though, aren't I? I know I'm a good listener. Mick said, Fat Judy said.

DAWN: You talk and you talk and you…

ALAN: I'm all ears. Try me. I will. I will listen. I'll learn to listen better. We could sit together, you and me, just sit down together and be all quiet and everything and you could do all the talking and I promise you, I promise you I won't speak, I won't say a single word. I'll just sit there and…

DAWN: Alan, you need to…

ALAN: And I won't interrupt you.

DAWN: You never let anyone get to the end of a sent…

ALAN: I promise I won't. I'll just sit there and you can tell me where I'm going wrong and how I need to change and I promise you I'll…

DAWN: It's not just about…

ALAN: I'll really, really try to listen to what you've got to say. I'll be much more…what's the word?…

DAWN: Alan, will you please just…

ALAN: Attentive.

They do not speak for a time.

DAWN: And Sean being away. I can't…

ALAN: I do know I can listen.

DAWN: I just can't set my mind to anything and…

ALAN: I really know I can.

DAWN: All day every day I'm anxious and I'm…

ALAN: This family is all I am. You, the girls. You're all I've got.

DAWN: And I'm tired of always being broke.

ALAN: But everybody's struggling at the moment…

DAWN: We're drowning in debt and we're…

ALAN: Then I'll drive a cab in the evenings. Or I'll…

DAWN: …and we can't repay what we owe and…

ALAN: I work hard! I've always worked hard! It's all I've ever done! But I'll work harder! If that's what it takes. I'll get two jobs, three jobs, I'll…

DAWN: I want an education. I want to become a more interesting person!

ALAN: You're interesting to *me*.

DAWN: And for you to be a more interesting person.

ALAN: I do my paintings.

DAWN: Not anymore!

ALAN: Because *she* said they were shite!

DAWN: And she was right, wasn't she!

A long silence.

I feel this pain. Here. It's like a constant hollow ache. Every hour of the day. I sometimes wake up in the middle night and I feel my heart is about to…

ALAN: You really think they're shite?

DAWN: I'm trying to tell you something!

ALAN: And I'm listening!

DAWN: I'm trying to explain…

ALAN: I am listening to you. Here I am, look. Listening. Go on! Say what you want to say.

DAWN: It's like there's something wrong with you!

ALAN: Well, there's something wrong with everyone, isn't there!

She says nothing for a time.

DAWN: All we ever talk about is the girls. What are we going to do when they've gone? They'll be gone before we know it. To be honest I am absolutely terrified of them going.

ALAN: What, and it just being you and me? You and me alone in the house?

DAWN: *(After a pause.)* Yes.

ALAN: That is the worst thing you could ever have said to me.

DAWN: I'm sorry.

ALAN: I don't know what to say to that.

DAWN: What would we talk about?

ALAN: If you ask me: what we all need right now is kindness and love and not more clever bloody conversations.

DAWN: I want to go to college. Study. Get out into the world. I want...

ALAN: Okay so listen to me: I'm making a decision. I'm making an important decision. I'm going to do it! I'm going to stop! Because it doesn't even make me happy! Because she's right, it costs us money we can't afford and it's making me boring and it's making me stupid. And so I'll just go ahead and do it!

DAWN: You'll do what?

ALAN: I'll bin the Skybox! Unsubscribe! Pack in the TV and the football and give up on the beers and I'll do something else with my time!

DAWN: I don't want my life to be exactly like this for the next forty years. I feel sad and cut off from life and I'm getting older...

ALAN: But you're still so gorgeous...

DAWN: What the hell does that matter?

ALAN: I'm the envy of the whole town!

DAWN: On Monday I felt so down. Couldn't face doing anything. Just watched TV. More reports of dead soldiers. I made some calls. It wasn't Sean's regiment. I thought about going into town but didn't want to see anyone. Talk to anyone. Didn't want anyone asking after him. Pitying me. Any more pity from people and I'll die. So I go outside as it's hot and I think I'll get a bit of sun. And I'm on the deckchair, feeling it on me and trying to calm the thoughts in my head but all I can think about is Sean out there and whether he's safe or not and then I start crying and I can't stop and then suddenly he's there, standing there, smiling down at me, asking if I'm alright.

ALAN: Who, Sean is? You're sort of hallucinating then?

DAWN: No, I'm seeing *him*! Next door! He's heard me crying and he's come through the gap in the fence and he asks if I want to come over for a drink and a chat and so I do and we come round here and he opens some wine and I say it's only eleven and he says let's live dangerously and so we get a bit drunk and we're talking and he's listening to me, like no one's ever listened to me before and he makes me laugh a bit and I tell him about Sean and he tells me how much he admires people who are prepared to fight and die for their country and then *I'm* crying and he's holding me and then he's telling me about their son that died one night while they were celebrating selling one of her paintings and before I know it he's telling me I'm the most beautiful woman he's ever seen and he's asking me if he can kiss me and then he's kissing me and then I'm kissing him and I can't stop myself from…

ALAN: I don't want to know!

DAWN: Something…came over me. Some terrible, unstoppable force and I know it was wrong but I felt more alive than I have done for years and years and…

They do not speak for a time.

Something came to me though: you ever wonder why people like him and her, why they send *their* kids off to university to read a few books, pass a few exams, become lawyers, doctors…

ALAN: Listen…

DAWN: While *we* send ours away to some desert to be blown to pieces by a load of…

ALAN: He's my son, Dawn! He'll be lucky!

DAWN: He is *not* your son!

ALAN: I'm the only father he's ever had.

81

DAWN: You've no idea how I feel!

ALAN: I brought up another man's child!

DAWN: And I have to be so grateful for it every single…

ALAN: I've only ever tried to be kind!

DAWN: And your kindness is killing me!

ALAN: Why are you being so…?

DAWN: Because it was you, it was you that made him go!

ALAN: We've got everything. You and me! You just don't see it!

DAWN: You told him it was better than working in that horrible pea factory or living off the…!

ALAN: Because of course it is!

DAWN: But they're dying every day out there!

ALAN: He's fighting for his country!

DAWN: But they're dying every day!

ALAN: He's doing something important with his…

DAWN: But they're still coming home in boxes!

ALAN: He could be wasting every day of his life in some tedious grind of a job…

DAWN: And how I wish he was!

ALAN: He'll come back home a man!

DAWN: And you know about that, do you?

ALAN: A proper man!

DAWN: Well, he won't come home!

ALAN: You don't know that.

DAWN: And even if he does he'll never be the same as he was! Look at Jackie's lad, look at Ian Baxter! One's drinking himself to an early grave and the other hangs himself in the woods. Why don't we ever see the sons of Prime Ministers going out there and then coming home depressed and suicidal? Why don't we ever hear about these rich kids blowing their own brains out because of what they've seen? It's always us, Alan! It's always people like us! It always has been and it always bloody will be!

ALAN: *(Holding her.)* Sean'll come home to us in six months' time with that big crazy laugh and that great wide smile and he'll be as right as rain. I promise you. He's not marked out to die. Look at me! Dawn, I promise you, I swear to you, I swear that boy will be coming home to us.

DAWN: You promise me?

ALAN: I promise.

DAWN: You swear on your life?

ALAN: I swear on all of our lives.

DAWN is in his arms, weeping.

OLIVER: *(Off.)* Emily, for the love of God, no!

Now EMILY and OLIVER come tearing into the room. He has been trying to prevent her from entering, dragging her back by the arm. She is too strong for him. She breaks free from his grasp but her momentum causes her to fall to the floor in a heap. ALAN and DAWN stare at her, bemused. Then EMILY drunkenly gets to her feet.

EMILY: My partner and I have been having a little meeting through there.

OLIVER: So sorry about this…

EMILY: And what we'd really, really appreciate is…if you would perhaps permit us to maybe…maybe to… I mean, if there's anything at all we can do for you then…

ALAN: There *is* something you could do for us…

EMILY: Anything, anything…

ALAN: The best thing you could do for us would be if you'd both just bugger off back to wherever it is you've come from.

EMILY sways.

SCENE 5

Several weeks later. OLIVER and EMILY are putting things away in boxes.
Crates stand around. This packing away goes on throughout the scene.
He is very urgent in what he's doing, she rather less so.

EMILY: The fact of the matter is, Oliver, I'm still not one
    hundred per cent convinced we're doing the right…

OLIVER: We discussed this and you agreed and so…

EMILY: I *sort of* agreed but…

OLIVER: Well, we're moving so…

EMILY: I haven't even seen this house so…

OLIVER: You'll love it. It's massive.

EMILY: Don't we have to give ourselves at least the chance
    to…

OLIVER: We're *never* going to settle here.

EMILY: We've only been here a few months…

OLIVER: And it's been a huge mistake…

EMILY: You have never in the whole time we've been together
    been anywhere near as assertive as…

OLIVER: I cannot live next door to this level of animosity
    any…

EMILY: Considering what you did I don't think it's been too
    bad so…

OLIVER: What do you mean?

EMILY: You murdered his cat.

OLIVER: I didn't *murder* his cat.

EMILY: Well, whatever you did that caused it to be currently
    mouldering away in our garden…

OLIVER: We just don't belong here.

EMILY: She's been doing it for days now. Just staring vacantly
    out of that window. I thought from the off they were a
    mismatch but I never for a moment sensed they were on
    the verge of separating. It must be so odd moving back

to the house you were brought up in. I'll put money on it there's a man involved.

OLIVER: What makes you say that?

EMILY: The woman clearly has itchy hips.

OLIVER: Didn't notice.

EMILY: Really?

OLIVER: I'm afraid I've always been rather oblivious to such things.

EMILY: I feel I ought to go round there.

OLIVER: You really needn't.

EMILY: She just stares out of that window all day.

OLIVER: It's sad, I agree, but…

EMILY: I keep thinking I ought to pop round to see him too.

OLIVER: I'm sure he's fine.

EMILY: And I feel so bad for those girls.

OLIVER: I'm sure it'll only be temporary.

EMILY: I do hope so.

OLIVER: If I could just put this here.

OLIVER continues to pack away.

EMILY: Aren't we paying those men to do all this?

OLIVER: They're on their lunch break and I'd like us to get away as soon as…

EMILY: I don't know quite how I feel about moving back to London.

OLIVER: You'll soon get used to the idea.

She watches him for a time.

EMILY: What's happened to you?

OLIVER: We just need to move, that's all…

EMILY: But we could easily rent another property here.

OLIVER: I am not renting, I am buying!

EMILY: Okay, okay…

OLIVER: And I want to live in London. I want my children to live in London and you, if you could just start being even a little bit honest with yourself, you yourself want to live in London

EMILY: Okay…

OLIVER: London is our home and it's what we know!

EMILY: You're being terribly shrill, Oliver.

OLIVER: *I'm* being terribly shrill?!

EMILY: Shrill, yes.

OLIVER: You're the one who's shrill.

EMILY: And how am I being shrill?

OLIVER: Shrill is your middle name.

EMILY: Who's the one being shrill now?

OLIVER: Listen, we have the money now so…

EMILY: I'm just uncomfortable with…

OLIVER: For God's sake, so you don't believe in inherited wealth, Emily, but what do you want me to do with it? She died, she left her money to us, she had way more money than we thought, what do I do? Do I just give it all away? Give it to the poor and needy? Or do we use it to help build a better life for ourselves?

EMILY: Why are you being so…?

OLIVER: I just want to get out of this place! I never wanted to move up here in the first place.

EMILY: Well, truth be told, I'm actually starting to feel more…

OLIVER: The locals despise us, the weather is awful, the school's like a borstal. We can now afford to put them both in some decent, independent school where they'll actually receive something bordering on an education…

EMILY: So exactly how much money did your mother…?

OLIVER: A substantial amount.

86

EMILY: Then why won't you tell me?

OLIVER: Because the accountants are still going through the figures.

EMILY: But your father worked for Barclays Bank!

OLIVER: That does not mean he was the Antichrist!

EMILY: You know what, I think it sort of does…

OLIVER: He was a good, hardworking, responsible…

EMILY: So hard to make a man understand the truth when his vast salary depends upon him *not* understanding it!

OLIVER: Not that again!

EMILY: Because the banks and the corporations….

OLIVER: Oh, Christ! The banks, the corporations! The banks, the corporations! It's all I ever hear you say… I mean, how much more of this am I expected to take!?

EMILY: They fund illegal wars and they trash the economy and…

OLIVER: The world is as it is, Emily!

EMILY: …it's everyone else who has to pick up the pieces!

OLIVER: And we just have to live in it as best we can!

EMILY: But it's all so wrong, so wrong!

OLIVER: So we're renting for a while and then we'll buy somewhere.

EMILY: How come *you're* suddenly making all the decisions?

OLIVER: Because for almost all my adult life I have let you make every single one of them and I have now finally…

EMILY: I feel like some cavewoman that's been clubbed over the head and…

OLIVER: I have now finally managed to grow myself a set of testicles.

EMILY: And does this seismic shift in you possibly have…

OLIVER: So get used to it!

EMILY: …have something to do with the death of your mother?

OLIVER: Maybe it does, maybe it doesn't.

He continues to pack things away at speed, moving about as if it's a race against time. She watches him.

EMILY: I just feel so bad, Oliver. Your mother and father represented everything I see as being…

OLIVER: Emily, for God' sake! It's *my* money, okay! If it makes you feel any better! It's *my* money! We're not married, are we? You're just my partner after all so relax about the money. You're obsessed with money! When I die I'll leave it to the kids and you can go straight into the workhouse or a convent if you want your precious conscience to remain clean. I'll buy a house in Highgate and you can live in a shed in the back garden and you can do your paintings and you can live off bread and water if that's what you want and we'll get you a hairshirt to wear and you can sleep on a straw mattress and we'll pay someone to come in and whip you a couple of times a day and any lack of comfort you require shall be yours for the asking but I am *not* living in the north of England for a second longer than I have to and I am now thankfully within a matter of hours of getting back to Planet Earth where I so obviously belong!

Stunned, she watches him as he continues.

EMILY: Highgate?

OLIVER: I've found us a place for six months. You'll like it.

EMILY: We can really afford Highgate now?

OLIVER: And then we'll buy somewhere.

EMILY: Then your parents must have been worth millions?

OLIVER: Life now is going to be a whole lot better for both of us.

EMILY: But what about the children?

OLIVER: They're going to have the best educations on offer. The future's going to be a big, nasty scrap for their

88

generation. Even more than it is now for this one. A real scramble for jobs, for housing. For everything. When they come of age, they'll need all the advantages they can get.

EMILY: But I just really don't…agree with it.

OLIVER: I'm afraid it's not all about you, is it?

EMILY: It's such an unfair…

OLIVER: I'm putting their names down.

She thinks about this for a time. They then continue packing things into the boxes and crates. After a time EMILY leaves for the front door with a box. She turns to him.

EMILY: Have to confess something to you: I seem to be finding this new Oliver Whetton strangely attractive.

She goes. OLIVER takes this in. Then continues. He is now holding a large framed photo of his mother in his hand. He looks at it sadly for a time. Fights the tears.

Now DAWN on. She has changed significantly over these last months. Her hair is dishevelled, she wears no make-up, is in a dirty tracksuit and is barefoot. She is clearly on some form of medication and has a somewhat glazed expression.

She watches him as he recovers and puts the framed photo into a box.

Then EMILY back on.

It would appear we have a visitor.

OLIVER turns.

An awkward silence.

OLIVER: Hello there?

No response.

EMILY: Can I get you anything? A cup of tea or…?

DAWN does not respond, looks around her, bewildered.

We have no milk but I can do you an Earl Grey?

No response.

Is everything alright?

No response.

Is there anything we can do for you?

No response.

"Well, I think I fancy a...yes... Why don't I put the kettle on?"

EMILY leaves.

DAWN: Saw the van outside.

OLIVER: That's right.

DAWN: Moving out, are you?

OLIVER: Back down south.

An awkward silence between them.

DAWN: Were you going to say goodbye?

OLIVER: Of course I was.

An awkward silence between them.

So...how have you...how have you been keeping?

No response.

I hear you're living with your mother now?

No response.

And is that okay or...?

More awkward silence, OLIVER wishing her far away.

My mother died last month actually.

No response.

Which is largely the reason we can afford to relocate.

No response.

Or to re-relocate, as it were.

He laughs nervously. No response.

I'm really sorry to hear about... I understand that you're having a bit of a...

DAWN: Living across the road now.

OLIVER: Yes.

An awkward silence.

And your husband…is he alright?

No response.

And your daughters are…?

DAWN: Spent a few days in hospital.

OLIVER: Did you?

An awkward silence.

You've been unwell then?

No response.

I hope it was…well…bearable?

A long, awkward silence. She is staring at him. He is very uncomfortable.

EMILY back on.

DAWN: There's something you need to know.

EMILY: Sorry?

DAWN: There's something you need to know.

OLIVER: We sort of need to be getting a move on actually.

EMILY: What do we need to know, darling?

DAWN, still in a state of confusion, looks around her.

Are you sure you're alright?

OLIVER: Seriously, I think we'd better be…

EMILY: Oh, my God, you poor thing, your feet are all bleeding. You've nothing at all on your… Let me…oh, let me take a look at this for you.

DAWN: There's something you need to know.

EMILY: Oliver, why don't you pop across to her mother's and get her shoes for her.

DAWN: There's something…there's something…

EMILY and OLIVER exchange puzzled looks.

OLIVER: Or shall I perhaps go and see if her husband is…?

EMILY: *(Mouthing.)* I think so.

DAWN: Don't go.

EMILY sits DAWN down and washes her dirty, muddy feet with a cloth.

There's something you need to know.

EMILY: You tell us then.

OLIVER: Listen, Emily…

DAWN: My heart is broken.

EMILY: How so?

DAWN: My heart is broken in a thousand pieces.

EMILY continues to tend to her feet.

I need to tell you.

Now some urgent knocking off. OLIVER goes off.

I need to tell people.

EMILY: Tell us, darling.

DAWN: A tank was on fire. His two best mates are in the tank. They're burning alive. Screaming. Can't get out. Bullets flying everywhere and Sean's across the road behind a wall, watching the tank, watching it burn…

EMILY: No, Dawn…

DAWN: So he runs over and he leaps onto the tank and he climbs up, and he pulls one of the lads out and he drags him, burning, screaming, starts dragging him back across the road where they save him. He saves the life of his mate. But as he rushes back to help the other lad he gets a bullet through the middle of his head. They're giving him a medal.

Now ALAN on in his postman's uniform. OLIVER after him.

ALAN: You really mustn't keep doing this, you know. Going out on your own. Your mum's out looking for you. Been knocking on every door. You mustn't just leave the house.

You need to tell her where you're going. And you need to keep your phone with you.

OLIVER: Everything okay?

DAWN: They're giving him a medal.

OLIVER: Because time really *is* of the essence, I'm afraid.

EMILY: I am so, so sorry.

DAWN slowly stands, rather unsteady, with EMILY helping her.

ALAN: This old lady's just called, love. She's seen our poster and she thinks she might have got Vince. She's not a hundred per cent certain but… He was in their garden and her son's managed to bring him into the house and it sounds like it really could be him. Me and the girls…we were going to head over there and…

DAWN slowly turns and looks at her husband.

So, maybe you'd like to…when I clock off…maybe we could all…?

EMILY: But Vince is dead, is he not?

ALAN: It's hard, love, to live in this world without a little bit of hope.

EMILY looks to OLIVER, who nods his head, shrugs. DAWN does not move, just looks around, dazed.

EMILY: Alan, please…if there's anything, anything at all we can do then…?

He does not respond. Waits for his wife to move.

OLIVER: *(To EMILY.)* We can think about heading off quite shortly actually. Are the children ready or…?

ALAN: *(To DAWN.)* It's such a beautiful day. So I thought maybe later we could all go for a walk along the canal. The girls have made some sandwiches…so maybe we could all… you know, get out and about. Sit together at the top lock. You know how much he always loved it up there.

No response.

We could just sit there and... I don't know...watch all the boats. Look out over the water.

DAWN slowly turns and looks at OLIVER. She opens her mouth to speak but no words come. She now looks back to ALAN as he smiles and holds out his hand towards her. She does not move.

The sound of birdsong, falling water.

OTHER TORBEN BETTS TITLES

Betts Plays One
A Listening Heaven / Mummies and Daddies / Clockwatching
9781840021769

Betts Plays Two
Incarcerator / Five Visions of the Faithful / Silence and Violence
/ The Last Days of Desire / The Biggleswades
9781840022001

Betts Plays Three
The Optimist / The Swing of Things / The Company Man
9781840028249

The Error Of Their Ways
9781840028010

Lie Of The Land
9781840028775

The Lunatic Queen
9781840025309

The Unconquered
9781840027235

Muswell Hill
9781849431378

WWW.OBERONBOOKS.COM

Follow us on www.twitter.com/@oberonbooks
& www.facebook.com/oberonbook